Harley-Davidson
Motor Company

**Recent Titles in
Corporations That Changed the World**

Toyota
K. Dennis Chambers

Harley-Davidson Motor Company

Missy Scott

Corporations That Changed the World

GREENWOOD PRESS
Westport, Connecticut • London

Library of Congress Cataloging-in-Publication Data

Scott, Missy.
  Harley-Davidson Motor Company / Missy Scott.
    p. cm. — (Corporations that changed the world, ISSN 1939–2486)
  Includes bibliographical references and index.
  ISBN-13: 978–0–313–34889–1 (alk. paper)
  1. Harley-Davidson Motor Company—History.   2. Motorcycle industry—
United States—History.   I. Title.
  HD9710.5.U54H3765   2008
  338.7'62922750973—dc22   2008018704

British Library Cataloguing in Publication Data is available.

Library of Congress Catalog Card Number: 2008018704
ISBN: 978–0–313–34889–1
ISSN: 1939–2486

First published in 2008

Greenwood Press, 88 Post Road West, Westport, CT 06881
An imprint of Greenwood Publishing Group, Inc.
www.greenwood.com

Printed in the United States of America

The paper used in this book complies with the
Permanent Paper Standard issued by the National
Information Standards Organization (Z39.48–1984).

10 9 8 7 6 5 4 3 2 1

To Ginny Rabbit

Contents

Preface

When I was 10 and living in Marine Corps project housing in Southern California in the 1950s, I had this boyfriend. He was 10, too. My mama, good Southern lady that she was, put him right at the top of her undesirable-playmates-for-my-daughter list because he was rowdy, went anywhere he pleased at all hours of the day and night, had black curly hair that was too long and rarely combed, wore old jeans and white undershirts (or worse, no shirt at all), and would spit anytime and anywhere he felt like it. Even in front of Mama. He was an outlaw.

Of course, I was forbidden to hang out with him. But that made him even more delicious, so we'd meet up secretly and spend hours riding our bicycles all over the project. He taught me this neat trick of attaching playing cards to the forks of the wheels with clothespins so the cards hit the spokes as the wheels went round and made it sound like a motor bike. It annoyed the neighbors and delighted us to no end. So we pinned on even more cards. Didn't make the bikes any louder, but the sound was definitely deeper, richer. You know, a here-we-come-and-we're-cool kind of sound. Both of us wanted real motorcycles badly. Outlaws at 10.

Ten years later, I was a college sophomore at a fine Virginia university, coming of age in the wild, defy-authority, question-everything world of the 1960s. The Beatles, Mick Jagger, Jimmy Hendrix, sit-ins, hippies, flower children, JFK, Vietnam, the Civil Rights Movement, protest marches, Yippies, Woodstock, sex, drugs, and rock and roll were turning everything upside down, inside out, and sideways. And I still wanted a motorcycle.

I got one, too. I emptied my savings account and bought a used, tricked-out Honda 305 Superhawk that had been stripped down and re-built with more Harley parts than Honda, including cylinders bored out for Harley pistons. It was a powerful machine and about the only thing left of it that was Honda was the name on the tank. Red with lots of chrome. It was fast, it was loud, and it was as close as I could come to a Harley on $350. I loved it. We won't discuss my mama's reaction.

Every spare moment that I wasn't in class or doing homework, I was out on that bike, cruising around the back streets of Williamsburg or flying down the Colonial Parkway, which ran along the James River, my face in the wind, totally reckless, feeling free. The speed limit on the Parkway was 45, but I figured that was only for cars, certainly not for bikes, and definitely not for me. And I often thought of that boy in California, even though I'd long forgotten his name. Was he doing time, studying to be a stockbroker, or was he roaring down the coast highway on a big Harley?

I have Bill Harley to thank for that shiny red jewel in the crown of my youth because he started it all. Like me and what's-his-name in California, he wanted more from his bicycle than what he had, but unlike us, his vision grew out of nothing except his own imagination and genius. He wanted a bicycle with a motor. People must have thought he was nuts. But young Bill Harley didn't care what they thought. He was an outlaw with a big dream.

He kept working on his designs for a small, gas-powered motor, and, with the help of his friend Arthur Davidson, finally built his first "motor bicycle." They didn't care when it turned out to be a semi-flop because it couldn't make it up hills without pedaling. They just took it back to the shop, enlisted the help of Arthur's brother Walter, redesigned the motor and made it bigger, and, in 1903, they produced a fully functional motor bicycle that made it up the hills on its own. It was black. The Davidsons' sister, Janet, hand painted the gold pin-striping and original Harley Davidson logo on the tank. It still had pedals, just in case. The dream had burst into full life, and there was no stopping it from that point on. Personal transportation was changing forever, people stopped snickering behind Bill Harley's back, and the legend began to stir.

The cadre of friends kept making their bikes bigger and more powerful, and in just a few years, Harleys were winning cross-country endurance races, as well as winning on the tracks where bikes hit 100 miles per hour and had no brakes. Police were chasing criminals on Harleys, and rural mail carriers traded their horses, mules, and bicycles for Harleys. Harleys were the machine of choice in both World Wars, and returning servicemen kept on riding them when they got home. Harley's growing reputation for fine craftsmanship, durability, and easy maintenance was building a brand loyalty the competition couldn't touch.

Over the years, new models and savvy marketing took Harley-Davidson more and more into the mainstream, and before long, every segment of society had die-hard Harley riders. The introduction of a series of touring bikes (aka Full Dressers) with their big saddle bags, windshields and full-fairings made open road, long-distance traveling comfortable and fun. While I was writing this book, I ran into a couple in their 70s in the parking lot of the grocery store, with matching Full Dressers, traveling south from Vermont. "Where are y'all headed?" I asked. "Who knows?" the wife said. "We were thinking about Florida, but might hang a right as we get further south and head West instead." Talk about outlaws! I kicked myself all the way home for not having my camera and some release forms with me so I could photograph them for the book.

OK. So now we *will* talk about the outlaws and the outlaw mystique that surrounds Harley. My definition of outlaw does not include bank robbers and car thieves. My outlaw is that freedom-seeking wild child in all of us, the part of us that is the rebel, the nonconformist, the part that bends the rules and sometimes breaks them just a little bit, the part that doesn't want to be stuffed into the same box as everybody else, the part that *must* do the very thing we're told absolutely *not* to do, even if only in our imaginations. Get the picture? I think that if more people would let that outlaw loose every now and then, there would be fewer prescriptions for Zoloft and Valium.

Motorcycles are just the thing to let the outlaw spirit fly, and they got a big boost in that direction with the 1953 release of *The Wild One,* starring Marlon Brando and Lee Marvin. It's true that Brando rode a Triumph in that movie, but Marvin rode a Harley. Suddenly, leather jackets, motorcycle boots, smirks, and attitudes were in. Motorcycle sales boomed. Motorcycle clubs of every size, shape, and description grew all over the country, and more and more weekend warriors left the office or assembly line behind and hit the road.

The rebellious spirit of the 1960s and motorcycles went together like peanut butter and jelly. Higher visibility of clubs like the Hells Angels and the Outlaws with their chopped Harleys, books like Hunter Thompson's *Hells Angels,* and a host of celebrities riding Harleys added to the aura. A string of biker movies, culminating in the 1969 classic *Easy Rider,* sealed it. It was all about freedom.

Top it off with the sound of a Harley. Attitude and then some! It's deep and resonant and powerful. Others, like Honda, have come close to duplicating it, but really and truly, the Harley sound is like no other. Once you've heard it, you'll always know there's a Harley coming long before it turns the corner.

Throughout the company's evolution, Harley-Davidson has held fast to the dream, and to its dedication to innovation. It has faced stiff competition from foreign brands, seen the bottom drop out of sales more than once, heard dire predictions of its imminent demise from financial pundits, looked down the barrel of bankruptcy, and, most recently, weathered a February 2007 workers' strike that sent its stock prices south. But it has always endured and come back stronger than ever.

This year, 2008, marks the 105th anniversary of Harley-Davidson, and the mother of all celebrations will be held in Milwaukee in August. Hundreds of thousands of Harley riders will stream into town in the well-orchestrated "Ride Home." All over the country, highways will be thundering with Harleys for as far as the eye can see. Miles and miles of Harleys, all heading home. Only a company that has changed the world in some way can bring that kind of magic and loyalty to their product and not only sustain it, but build it over the generations. Even people who don't like Harleys often have to admit, "there's just something about a Harley."

Some Motorcycle Slang to Get You Going

Keep the shiny side up—Have a good trip.
Keep the dirty side down—Also means have a good trip, but from a
      different perspective.
Light the fire—Start the engine.

So let's get to it. Let's take the Harley journey together, get our faces in the wind, and have a good ride. But before we begin, I'm giving you a little assignment. Get those movies—*The Wild One* and *Easy Rider*. I don't care if you've seen them before. Watch them again. Your journey will be so much richer for it.

Whenever you're ready, light the fire. And keep the shiny side up.

Acknowledgments

Some of the photos in this book are from my own collection and are noted as such. Some were given to me years ago by relatives and friends who knew my passion for motorcycles. Others I bought at swap meets or shows. The ones from my collection that I put in the book have no identifying material on the back as to ownership and I have used them in good faith to enrich the experience of our readers. Please forgive me if I have unknowingly stepped on any toes.

My deepest thanks to:

Ginger Scott, my sister, friend, supporter and cheerleader whose insights on design and structure really helped me shape this book. Be sure to read her book on Google in the Corporations That Changed the World series.

Jeff Olson, Senior Acquisitions Editor at Greenwood. More than a fine editor. A friend and mentor with just the right wise words at just the right moment. After all these months, you're a shoo-in for sainthood.

Dean Strong, my cousin who honored the muse.

Lynn Grosz, dear unconditional friend and confidant, always there for me no matter what mood I was in.

Uri Levi, artist and dreamer who cheered me on despite his own challenges.

Joe and Jennifer Heller, longtime biker friends who answered at least a thousand questions that added so many fine details to the book.

Bill Jackson, Harley-Davidson Archivist and Keeper of the Flame, who answered all my questions with such patience and kindness. A lovely man.

Don Argento, Marketing Director at the Motorcycle Hall of Fame Museum, who made things happen fast at just the right time. If you're ever anywhere near Pickerington, Ohio, be sure to visit the museum. And, while you're there, look up Don and give him a big hug from me.

Randy Simpson at Milwaukee Iron, who took me on a wonderful journey into the world of custom-built motorcycles. Very nice man with a big heart.

Robert W. Dye, Photography Manager at Elvis Presley Enterprises, Inc/Graceland, who told me some great stories about Elvis, as well as some great stories from his own father, a photographer, who photographed Elvis many, many times. Robert has published three exquisitely beautiful historical pictorial books of his own and has another in the works.

Margaret Maybury at Greenwood who connected me up with good people and good information, and gave me some great tips for transplanting my irises. You're a sweetie and your enthusiasm and good cheer is contagious.

Jennifer Boelter at Apex CoVantage who, with her merry band of artists, put all the pieces together to make this a book and helped me through the process of page proofs with incredible patience and good humor. You're a princess!

Ben Brown, my outlaw doc, for supporting and encouraging me, for helping me along a sometimes bumpy path and, most of all, for trusting me.

Reynolds Mansson, M2 MotoMedia, old biker friend from the 1960s who turned me on to some very cool Harley people to talk to for the book.

Pat Graham-Block, who got the ball rolling.

The brotherhood of bikers who know the meaning of camaraderie and loyalty, who never let a brother or sister down and who do their own part in their own way to make the world a better place.

And to all you modern-day outlaws out there, even if you have to put on a coat and tie, or eye makeup and stilettos in your day jobs. Without outlaws we'd still be living in caves. Ride your dreams and let it rip, boys and girls!

Chapter 1

In the Beginning

Milwaukee, Wisconsin, in the late 1800s and early 1900s was a bustling, thriving child of the Industrial Revolution, nestled on the shores of Lake Michigan, growing by leaps and bounds. In 1880, the year that William S. Harley was born, the population was over 115,000. By the time the first Harley-Davidson motorcycle was sold in 1903, the population had shot up to over 300,000. Plentiful jobs in rapidly expanding milling and manufacturing industries and in the breweries that would make Milwaukee famous attracted people from all over the country, especially new immigrants to the United States. Many German immigrants settled there, and in the early twentieth century, there were more German-speaking people and German-language newspapers in the city than English. Milwaukee, along with New York City, had the largest foreign-born population of any city in America. Others came as well—from Poland, Ireland, Scotland, England, and Italy, along with a smattering of Central and Eastern European Jews. Among all those new arrivals were the Harleys from England and the Davidsons from Scotland.

LIFE WAS VERY DIFFERENT THEN

If you hopped into a time machine and went back to those days, you might not like it very much. There were no computers, no cell phones, no iPods, no television, no movies, and very little radio. Telephones were around, but only in the city and areas close to the city, and there was no such thing as a private line. You'd be lucky to be on a line with only 15 other people. Even into the early 1960s, few private lines were available out in the rural areas. You could go crazy waiting while someone on a four-party line rattled on about her gall bladder surgery. That's right. Anybody could listen in at any time, so you dared not talk about anything much more controversial than the weather. Those were not times for discussing high-level business deals over the phone unless you wanted the entire city of Milwaukee to know about it within five minutes.

Like telephones, electricity was available in the city and nearby but nonexistent in the rural areas. Country folk either went to bed when it got dark or lit their homes with candles and kerosene lamps. In some cases, the only light was an open fireplace. Remember Abe Lincoln studying and reading by the light of the fireplace? In both city and country, people cooked their food and heated their homes with wood or coal stoves. Air conditioning in the summertime meant opening the windows. Very few homes outside the city had any kind of indoor plumbing. That meant hauling water by hand from a spring or hand-dug well, and answering nature's call with a quick run to the outhouse. No washers and dryers or microwaves or vacuum cleaners. Life was hard for a lot of people, especially in the winter when the fierce, icy winds blew in off Lake Michigan. It's no wonder people didn't live as long as they do today, and often died from ailments that are easily treated now.

TRANSPORTATION WAS VERY DIFFERENT, TOO

There were no paved roads except in the city, and those were brick, cobblestone, or logs laid side-by-side, then covered with tar and gravel. Not a smooth ride for any vehicle, and slick as glass when it rained. Outside the city, it was all dirt roads, sometimes with a bit of gravel, but they were mostly rutted tracks that turned into sucking mud in the rain and snow. Remember now, there were no bulldozers or other kinds of equipment to maintain roads like we have now. Any road improvements were made by hand—back-breaking work with shovel, pick, rake, and lots of sweat. The gravel was hauled in wagons pulled by mules or oxen, unloaded by hand, then hand-spread on the roads. No dump trucks. Most of the time, it wasn't worth all the trouble, and people just made do.

There were a few thousand motorized or steam-powered vehicles around the United States back then—both automobiles and very simple motorized bicycles. They were expensive and mostly toys for rich folks. They were noisy, smelly, and very cranky, prone to breaking down in the middle of a trip or refusing to start at all. So most people depended on horses, bicycles, or their own two feet to get around. Within the city, you could catch a ride to another part of town on one of the electric trolley cars. Goods for the shops and materials for the industries and breweries were delivered by wagons drawn by horses or oxen. Finished goods produced in Milwaukee headed out to their destinations in the same way. Trains carried goods, raw materials, and people longer distances between cities, and when weather permitted, ships and barges shuttled people and products back and forth across Lake Michigan. But lake travel was always at the mercy of the weather and the seasons. The lake became treacherous during storms, and impassable when frozen in winter, and many ships and lives were lost over the years.

FOOD FOR BODY AND SOUL

Food was fresh, brought in daily from the outlying farms during the growing season. Fish caught in Lake Michigan sold out the same day at the fishmongers' shops or off the backs of the fish wagons that traveled through the neighborhoods. Horse-drawn wagons delivered milk straight from the cow in glass bottles to the doorstep before dawn. Every day, wagons made the rounds with the ice used in those big, tin-lined wooded refrigerators known as "ice boxes." Most folks stocked up for winter by canning the fresh produce during the summer and making jams and jellies with fruit right off the tree. Commercial canneries supplied those that weren't into do-it-yourself, but store-bought canned goods were expensive and most people considered them a luxurious treat for special occasions. Fresh fish, meat, poultry, and eggs were pretty much available year round.

And there was plenty of fun to be had, even for those people who worked long hours in the factories and breweries. Fishing was a very popular pastime, even for those with little money since all you needed was a pole, a line, and a bit of bait. For those who could afford it, golf was hugely popular. And, of course, the bicycle provided hours of adventures around the city, and out along country lanes.

In the city, there was theater and music, and sometimes a traveling opera or stage show came to town. In areas of the city where the immigrants settled into tight-knit communities, the pubs were meeting places, more for socializing than for drinking. The markets were great places to catch up with the latest news from home or what was happening around the neighborhoods. In both city and countryside, families were closer and spent more time together. It wasn't just catching up on the day at dinnertime but spending time talking and laughing and singing and passing down the stories of the generations. Kids played outside, got dirty, made mud pies, rode bicycles, fished, and formed lifetime friendships. Entertainment was much simpler than it is today, and perhaps richer in that simplicity. Who can say?

After reading all this you might be thinking, "Wow, life was hard and sort of boring back then." But keep in mind that most people didn't see it that way. It was what they knew, and, as each new "convenience" appeared on the scene, they saw progress forward. In many ways, it was better than what they had lived before. This was especially true of the immigrants who had come to America seeking a better life and found it in Milwaukee. It certainly was true of Bill Harley's parents and of the Davidson brothers' grandparents and their children. Thank goodness they came, and they stayed, and they gave us those boys who would grow up to create the motorcycles so loved around the world.

Chapter 2

Meet the Founders: Building the Dream Team

Bill Harley and the Davidson brothers were born and raised in Milwaukee, the first generation American-born children of their immigrant parents. The families lived next door to each other, and Bill and Arthur Davidson were friends almost from day one. They played together, fished together, played golf together, and spent endless hours riding their bicycles here, there, and yon. Even as youngsters, they loved tinkering around with things. They loved studying how things worked and coming up with one wild idea after another to make something bigger, better, faster, or creating some new contraption altogether. They fiddled around, making modifications to their bicycles, and they even built a couple from scratch when they got a little older. They were both very bright, very talented, and very practical. Their enthusiasm was infectious, and, as their vision of a motorized bicycle grew and they got serious about actually building one, the other Davidson brothers were drawn, one by one, under the spell. Let's meet them all now.

WILLIAM S. HARLEY

Bill Harley was born in 1880, one of seven children. He had two brothers and four sisters. Somewhat shy and reserved, he inherited the strong work ethic of his parents and set definite goals for himself, determined to be successful at anything he put his hand to. By age 15, he was working in a bicycle factory.

He worked on the assembly floor, where he learned about frames and fittings for bicycles. A couple of years later, he took an apprenticeship in drafting at the same metal fabrication plant where Arthur worked as an apprentice patternmaker. This early experience laid the foundation for his ability to design the kinds of bike frames that could handle an engine—frames that put the stamp of unique form and function on every Harley-Davidson motorcycle to come.

It also fueled his desire to learn more about engineering and design. In 1903, after the first 3 official Harley-Davidson motorcycles had been sold, he enrolled in the University of Wisconsin engineering program. He worked his way through school waiting tables and working as a draftsman. When he graduated, he returned to Milwaukee and to the fledgling company and took on the role of chief engineer and treasurer. He was the only one of the four founders with a college degree.

Because he was an avid rider himself, he tested out all of his designs personally, and even ran a few endurance races. His focus was always on performance, durability, efficiency, and what his customers might want. As the business grew, and more and more people were riding Harleys, he made a point of taking the ride to rallies like the big one in Daytona Beach to meet riders from all over the world and hear what they had to say. The ideas and comments he gathered at these meet-ups were always at the forefront of his mind when he went back to the drafting table. Not only *meeting* the needs of the riding public but *anticipating* them was the cornerstone of the business from the very beginning. As you will see as the story unfolds, the company lost sight of this principle for a time after all the founders had died, and it cost them dearly. But a new band of visionaries revived it in the nick of time and it endures to this day.

He was not all work and no play, however. He still hunted, fished, and played golf with his friends, especially Arthur. In later years, as the bikes got bigger and sidecars were added, it was not unusual for the two of them to come home with sidecars piled high with fish caught in Lake Michigan.

He and his wife, Anna, raised three children, and he maintained his position of chief engineer and treasurer at Harley-Davidson until his death from heart failure in 1943.

ARTHUR DAVIDSON

Arthur Davidson was born in 1881, one of six children, and the youngest of the three brothers that became the founders of Harley-Davidson along with Bill Harley. Arthur went to work at the same bicycle factory as Bill. While Bill was designing, Arthur was working as a patternmaker, a specialty skill that he would bring to their young company in the very early days.

Unlike Bill, Arthur was outgoing and chatty, loved telling stories and meeting new people. So, even though you'd think his permanent role in the company would have been more in design and patternmaking, he took up the post of secretary and general sales manager. His personality suited the role to a T, and his first major project was setting up dealerships.

He believed that the company needed to do more than just make motorcycles if they were to continue to expand as they envisioned. Arthur knew the bikes were great. But how could they sell if nobody knew about them? So he developed advertising campaigns to create brand recognition and keep Harley-Davidson motorcycles in the public eye and in high demand. He came up with several other innovative ideas that helped launch the company into a rapid period of growth, including:

- Setting up a school to train certified Harley mechanics.
- Creating a strong alliance with the American Motorcyclist Association, whose members included both industry representatives and the riding public.
- Organizing a finance company for Harley buyers as installment buying became more and more popular.

When Arthur wasn't working at the company or visiting his dealers or dreaming up yet another way to promote their motorcycles, he was hunting and fishing and golfing with his best friend, Bill. In his later years, he began raising prize-winning Guernsey cattle at his farm outside Milwaukee, and spent more and more time there after World War II.

He was generous with his money, and he supported many worthy causes. His own personal philanthropy, and that of his brother, Walter, set the stage for the charitable foundations and trusts that the Harley-Davidson Motor Company would establish over the years.

He and his wife, Clara, raised three children, and he remained hands-on at the company until 1950, when he and his wife died in a car wreck.

Patternmakers and Machinists

Patternmakers, like Arthur, created the full-scale patterns for each of the pieces that would make up a finished product. Sometimes, they would even make a model of it from wood or clay. The pattern went to the machinists, like Walter, who used the metalworking tools to create the part from the raw materials. So, let's say Bill has just done the drawing for the casing to be bolted to the bike frame to hold the engine. He'd give that drawing to Arthur, who would make the life-size pattern. Arthur would hand that pattern off to Walter, who would create the actual casing using a combination of handwork and machine tools to complete the job.

WALTER DAVIDSON

Walter Davidson was born in 1876, and, as a very young man, went to work for a railroad company in the southwestern United States. He was a skilled mechanic and machinist, and he was sort of snookered into joining the young motorcycle company. He had come back to Milwaukee for his older brother's wedding, and Bill and Arthur asked him if he'd like to come have a ride on their new motor bicycle. What they didn't tell him was that he'd have to put it together first. As it turned out, he was so enchanted with this new machine that he quit his railroad job and joined the company. He went to work as a machinist at a local plant, and worked on the bikes in the evenings and on weekends.

He became the company president and set high standards for quality and excellence in the machines that were produced. Like the rest of the founders, his focus was on customer satisfaction, and he considered the buying public his "employer." He was both business and money savvy, and had a reputation for using materials and resources efficiently and effectively. He was quite frugal managing the company funds, but he freely gave his own money to charity.

He loved building and racing bicycles as a young man. That love was transferred to motorcycles. He scored the company's first significant racing victory in 1908 when he won a medal in a big New York endurance race. His performance boosted the Harley-Davidson name in the public eye and added yet another selling point for the sales teams and dealerships that Arthur was busily organizing.

He and his wife, Emma, had three sons. He was still running the company when he died in 1942.

The Start of a Motorcycle Dynasty

Many of the founders' children followed their dads into the company, and some of the Davidson descendants are still with the company today. The Harley and Davidson families have remained close over the years, even as they scattered to other parts of Milwaukee or other parts of the country and no longer live right next door to each other.

WILLIAM DAVIDSON

William Davidson was born in 1870, the oldest of the founders and the last to join the group. As soon as he was old enough, he went to work for the Milwaukee Road railroad company where became a skilled machinist and toolmaker. As the demand for Harleys grew, he quit his job at the railroad and joined the company as vice president and works manager. He also bought all the machinery to make the parts and tools the expanding company needed to keep growing.

In the early days, he did most of the hiring and had a good eye for picking the right people for the jobs at hand. He spent as much time on the shop floor as he did in his office, and his door was always open to anyone who cared to drop by. It was an early form of the "open-door" management style that other companies would later adopt and is the foundation of Harley-Davidson management today.

He truly listened to what his employees had to say, and this close working relationship led to new and more efficient ideas for parts production and assembly techniques. Under his guidance and in partnership with his employees, many of the processes involved in building motor-cycles were streamlined and improved.

In 1937, employees started the process of forming a union, which the company fought unsuccessfully. William, especially, was upset and disillusioned. Why would they want to unionize when management and employees all seemed to work together so harmoniously? Heartbroken, he signed the agreement allowing the union. He died two days after the ink was dry.

THE POWER OF THE DREAM

Something very interesting happens when a strong, new idea is born. It happened with Bill Harley's idea for a motorized bicycle. He loved cycling, but he felt the whole experience would be easier and more fun if he didn't have to pedal. He also had a strong notion that other people just might feel the same way. There could be a good market for such a machine. He knew it could be done because there were already motorized bicycles in Europe, and a few in the United States. But Bill knew he could make them better!

So, he thought about it and the idea grew. When he talked to Arthur about it, Arthur got excited, too, especially about the business angle, and it grew some more. As the idea became clearer and more focused, and they got down to the serious business of actually designing a motorized bicycle, other people appeared at just the right time with the resources and know-how to move things along. The idea got even bigger and stronger. After they built their first bike, and decided what needed to be changed to make it work better, new people and resources showed up with solutions and suggestions. When they needed someone to design the parts and assemble the bikes, Walter joined the company. When they needed someone to design and build the machines to make the parts and run the shop, William joined the company. The idea became a physical reality when they sold their first three bikes in 1903. At that point, Arthur turned his "people skills" toward setting up dealerships to sell the bikes, training the salespeople, and building the brand through advertising. So, part two of the idea—selling a product that would enhance the lives of others—also became a physical reality.

Isn't it amazing how that little glimmer of an idea in Bill Harley's head grew brighter and brighter as the enthusiasm grew? Each person he attracted to himself added to it until all the pieces of the tapestry were complete—design, production, marketing—and became the Harley-Davidson Motor Company.

Chapter 3

Born in a Basement

When Bill and Arthur were just boys, bicycles were the newest craze. They were not expensive, made getting around a lot easier and more fun, and just about everybody had one. Bill and Arthur were no exceptions and quickly became fanatical fans of bicycling in any form, including racing.

Bicycle racing was a very popular sport, and Bill and Arthur may have seen their first gasoline engine at one of those races. A bike with a clip-on engine served as the pace bike to start the races—just like the pace car at Indianapolis today. You can just imagine what ideas started sprouting in those fertile young minds when they saw it.

The First Motorcycles

Howard Roper developed a coal-powered, steam-engine motorcycle in 1867, and Gottlieb Daimler, a German, developed a gas-powered engine in 1885, which he attached to a wooden bicycle frame.

It doesn't really matter where they saw the first one. They started playing around with making one of their own. Their new hobby was making a gasoline engine. As luck would have it, a coworker at the fabricating plant who had emigrated from Germany had blueprints for the small French DeDion-Bouton engine. This was the same clip-on engine used on the pace bikes. It was first introduced in Paris by the Aster Company in 1895.

The drawings helped them think about how they could create their own engine, and they came up with a plan. Now it was time to put all the pieces together. But first they had to make the pieces. In 1901 there was no NAPA store where they could just go buy parts. They all had to be made from scratch. Bill and Arthur didn't have sophisticated machining tools like the Aster Company, so they had to make do with the tools they had on hand. Arthur called on his friend, Ole Evinrude, who knew a lot about gasoline engines, to help create any other parts they needed. Having seen the pace bikes, they knew how everything was supposed to fit together.

The Pace Bikes

U.S. engineer Oscar Hedstrom built the first pacer to train bicyclists for marathons in the early 1900s. In 1901, George Hendee built the first plant to produce them in Springfield, Massachusetts. Hedstrom and Hendee's company was Indian Motorcycle Company, and it grew to be a powerful force in motorcycle history until it was dethroned by Harley-Davidson.

They set up shop in the Davidson's basement and got to work cobbling together their motor bicycle.

They used a heavyweight bicycle frame and wheels and made a long, narrow rectangular tank fit on the top bar of the frame to hold the gasoline. They used a soup can for the basic carburetor but ran into problems getting the fuel flow right. Evinrude helped them re-engineer their soup can so they had a working carburetor. He also rigged up a kind of spark plug that ended up being about the size of an egg—not even a vague resemblance to the spark plugs we know today. By the way, Ole went on to found his own company in 1909, building out-board motors for boats. Evinrude is still a respected company today. Clearly, there was a lot of talent and innovation in Milwaukee in the early 1900s.

They experimented with their project over the next year or so, but soon realized that they needed someone with more mechanical ability. Enter Arthur's brother, Walter. They'd been keeping Walter up to date on things by mail while he was out west working for the railroad, and he was fascinated by it. Then came big brother William's wedding, Walter came home for it, and you know the rest of that story. Things really started to move forward after Walter joined the company. Another friend also let them use his workshop that had a lathe for shaping the parts, a drill press, and other tools they needed. Before long, they had built their first motor bicycle.

TIME TO HIT THE ROAD

Road testing began in earnest and was both frustrating and fruitful. The bike did fairly well on the flats, but with only about 2 horsepower, it couldn't make it up the hills without pedaling. Top speed was about 25 miles per hour. They learned a lot from this first attempt and went back to the drawing board.

Bill got busy making his own set of drawings for a more powerful engine based on the DeDion plans. Arthur was, no doubt, looking over his shoulder the whole time, making suggestions based on his experience as a patternmaker. You can design just about anything on paper, but will

it work in real life? Bill designed a new engine that was bigger than the DeDion, and Arthur got busy making the patterns for the parts.

For Gearheads

The DeDion engine was a single-cylinder, four-stroke engine (2½-inch bore and 2½-inch stroke), producing about 2 horsepower. Bill Harley's beefed up design was a 3⅛-inch bore and 3½-inch stroke, with heavier-duty flywheels and castings. With the longer stroke, it was actually more like a racer. It produced about 3 horsepower.

Another test run with the new, more powerful engine, was successful. The frame of the bike was another matter, however, and was in a shambles from the stress and demands of the bigger engine. The traditional diamond-shaped frame was discarded and replaced with a loop frame that cradled the whole engine assembly. It was a perfect example of form following function—a design created for a specific performance. The loop frame became the standard for all the Harleys that followed for many years.

When all the pieces came together, Bill and Arthur and Walter had a simple machine, with clean lines, no fenders, and pedals to get the bike started. The difference between this bike and their earlier ones was that this one went everywhere under its own power, even up the steepest hill in Milwaukee. They had built a motorcycle.

MOTORCYCLES FOR SALE

About this time, it became obvious they'd outgrown their basement workshop. It was also obvious that they were serious about producing bikes to sell, so the Davidsons' Dad built them a 10 foot by 15 foot shed in the back yard. Sister Janet painted the name on the door—Harley Davidson Motor Co. Who knows why it wasn't Davidson Harley? After all, there were three Davidsons and only one Harley. Maybe they thought Harley Davidson was just more "musical," or flowed better. Whatever the name on the door of their new shop, Mama Davidson was probably very relieved to have those boys and their tools and their noise and their mess out of her basement. And proud of them, too.

The elder Davidson installed a lathe and drill press in the new shop, and Bill, Arthur, and Walter got busy building two more motorcycles. They already had buyers for all three who paid for the bikes in advance. The bikes cost $200—pricey for those days. That translates to a little over $5,000 in 2008 dollars. Their sales brochure made a point of saying their bikes were not meant to be cheap, but were meant to last. Their rigorous, almost brutal, testing of their first real prototype had shown the bikes to be tough and reliable. Reliable was the key word, too, because there were quite a few

much cheaper motorized bikes around that weren't worth a darn. They were produced quickly to take advantage of the growing market without much thought to durability. The Harleys, however, were robust and tough, and, as the word got out, more orders started coming in. They were on their way.

The 1903 Harley

The first production Harley had Bill's modified DeDion engine, 26.8 cc displacement, a belt drive, and a one-gallon gas tank. It held one quart of oil, and had a hand pump to manually lubricate the engine. There were no recirculating oil pumps back then. It had no brakes. To stop it, you pedaled backwards. It was black, with the Harley Davidson name and pin striping in gold, hand-painted by Janet Davidson. Henry Meyer, a friend of Bill and Arthur, bought one of the first ones. He later sold it, and it passed through at least five different owners over the course of the years. When last heard of in 1913, it had clocked over 100,000 miles with no major repairs, no parts replacement, and was still going strong. It still even had the original bearings.

Somehow, the very first 1903 Harley with serial #1 made its way back to Milwaukee and is now in the front lobby of Harley-Davidson headquarters. It came home.

The 1903 Harley. Courtesy of Harley-Davidson Archives. Copyright Harley-Davidson.

It's no secret that Bill and Arthur didn't come up with a lot of their ideas all on their own. There were two other fairly successful companies out there by the time they sold their first bikes. Excelsior and Indian topped the list with Pierce, Merkel, Schickel, and Thor sharing the rest of the market. What they *did* do was put their own distinctive mark on every single piece of every single bike they made. The frames were sturdier, and all the parts were heavier and stronger than anything out there. Their bikes were built to be tough, require minimal maintenance, and give excellent service over the long haul. This business and production philosophy was the foundation of Harley-Davidson from day one.

In late 1903, Bill left for college at the University of Wisconsin to study engineering. Arthur and Walter held down the fort, but Bill kept in touch and visited as often as he could. As new ideas popped into his head, he passed them along to his partners. He stayed as active in the business as he could while balancing school and work.

As we'll see in the next chapter, production never skipped a beat, the business grew, and the Harley reach extended further and further. When Bill returned full-time in 1908, their fledgling project had become a thriving enterprise with an expanding group of delighted and loyal Harley owners. With Bill back home, full of new knowledge, new skills, and a head full of ideas, a bright new era of innovation was about to dawn. Some of the most memorable moments in motorcycle history were waiting in the wings.

Timeline for the Early Days

Late 1880s–1901	Some European companies were already producing motorized bicycles. A couple of American companies like Indian and Excelsior were producing quality bikes for the enthusiast market. A few smaller companies were making cheap imitations that didn't hold up.
	Bill Harley and Arthur Davidson knew about them, and became determined to build their own, only better.
1900–1901	Sometime during this period, Bill and Arthur were given the plans for the DeDion engine.
1901–1903	Bill and Arthur began making parts based on the DeDion plans, but realized they needed more skilled mechanical help, so they conned Walter Davidson into joining the company.

With Walter's help, they built their first motorized bicycle. It proved to be underpowered, with a weak frame, so it was totally redesigned.

1903   They moved their operation into the backyard workshop built for them by the Davidsons' Dad.

Testing of the new model was successful, and they produced their first three bikes, all pre-sold.

Bill Harley went off to engineering school at the University of Wisconsin, while production continued at home.

Transportation took a huge leap in 1903. Bill, Arthur, and Walter sold their first official Harley-Davidson motorcycles, Henry Ford introduced the Model A Ford automobile, and the Wright Brothers made the first manned flight at Kitty Hawk, North Carolina.

Chapter 4

There's No Stoppin' Us Now: The Growing Years, 1904–1908

In 1904, the Motor Company, as the founders referred to it, produced eight more bikes. That's not many, but remember: Each part of each bike was made by hand, and each bike was put together by hand. It was a time-consuming process. There were only so many hands doing the work once Bill left for college, and both Arthur and Walter were still holding down full-time day jobs. William had not joined them yet. They worked late into the night after work, and most all of every weekend. Even though their funds and work space were limited, they hired some part-timers to help out occasionally. In later years, Walter would look back on those days when "we worked every day, Sunday included, until at least 10 o'clock at night. I remember it was an event when we quit work on Christmas night at 8 o'clock to attend a family reunion."[1]

The size of their little shop expanded during this time, too, but it was obvious they needed an even bigger building than the Davidsons' backyard could handle. So they started shopping around for a site. They picked a spot on what is now Juneau Avenue in Milwaukee, where Harley-Davidson headquarters still stands today. Financing came from a reclusive beekeeper uncle, James McLay. Some accounts of the deal say the founders asked him for a loan to back them. But there's also the tale of the "Honey Uncle" recounted by Walter's granddaughter, Jean Davidson, in her book, *Jean Davidson's Harley-Davidson Family Album*. She says the founders kept all their sales profits in a jar rather than a bank, and somehow the money was stolen. When McLay heard what happened, he sent them a big check that more than covered what they needed.[2]

The new building, 28 feet by 80 feet, hit a snag right at the beginning. They had just framed it out when the railroad company told them the building extended a couple of feet onto their land. Yikes! Now what? Cool-headed, methodical Walter simply went and fetched a dozen or so strong helpers who literally picked the whole building up and moved it the necessary distance. They moved their operation into the new digs in

1906. Both Walter and Arthur had quit their day jobs shortly before the move, and big brother William quit his job with the railroad to join them in early 1907. They hired six full-time workers, and started turning out about one motorcycle a week. Every bike got a full test run by one of the founders before it got the OK for delivery. Thorough test runs continued as standard procedure even as production increased year by year.

By 1907, the size of the building doubled, the workforce rose to 18 and they were able to produce 150 motorcycles that year. Even though Bill Harley was still away at school, the company became an official corporation that same year. Walter became president, Bill the chief engineer and treasurer, Arthur the sales manager and secretary, and William vice president and works manager. Each of the founders took equal shares of stock.

The Open-Door Management Policy

From the very beginning, William encouraged a close working relationship with employees and spent more time on the production floor than in his office. He made it known that he respected their skill and valued their input about procedures and processes. He told them his door was always open to them. From this easy and respected partnership came many innovations in production that increased company efficiency and the quality of their motorcycles.

In those early days, their new titles only meant they had certain responsibilities within the company. Basically, everybody did a little bit of everything, and if one of them learned a new skill, they taught it to everyone, including all the employees. William had an excellent relationship with all the employees, and he invited their suggestions for ways to make production more efficient. Founders and employees together created design, tooling, and production techniques that improved the breed across the board.

THE BIKES EVOLVED TOO

The 1904–1905 bikes were pretty much the same as the 1903 model—black with gold pin-striping and the Harley-Davidson logo on the tank. Same engine. The 1906 models were a different story altogether. In addition to the basic black, the company added the color gray with red detailing, ushering in the era of the Silent Grey Fellow.

The bikes in those days had two speeds. Go or go not, as Yoda might say. There was neither clutch nor brake pedal. To get the engine

1906 Silent Grey Fellow. Courtesy of the Motorcycle Hall of Fame Museum.

Why the Silent Grey Fellow? What a Name for a Motorcycle

There are two stories about how that name came to be. One follows the line that the "silent" part referred to the muffler system that made the bikes quieter than others on the market. This was part of the Motor Company's ad campaign portraying the company as a responsible, conscientious member of the community. The "grey" of course, referred to the color. The "fellow" made it a kind of companionable buddy out there on the road.

Jean Davidson's tale goes that the bike was given Bill Harley's nickname—the Silent Grey Fellow—an endearing title bestowed by the Davidson brothers because of his shy nature and premature grey hair.[a] However it came by its name, the Silent Grey Fellow became the foundation bike and saw many changes over the years.

[a]Jean Davidson, *Jean Davidson's Harley-Davidson Family Album* (Stillwater, MN: Voyageur Press, 2003), p. 27.

started, you connected the battery ignition, pedaled like mad while the bike was still on the stand, then pushed off when the engine got going. The only way to modulate the speed somewhat was by a spring-loaded lever attached to the leather drive belt that adjusted the tension against the rear wheel. This adjusted the speed and served as the brakes along with back-pedaling. It worked only marginally well under the best of circumstances, and not at all in rainy weather when the belt got wet and slick. It probably made for a sort of jerky, lurching ride on the best of days. Even though it was an annoying problem sometimes, the leather drive belt would stick around for a few more years. It didn't seem to be slowing down sales any, and Silent Grey Fellows kept going out the door. They helped firmly establish Harley's reputation for a reasonably priced, reliable bike.

There was a bigger problem that needed attention first. The rigid-frame front end made for a bone-rattling ride and somewhat challenging steering, especially on bumpy surfaces. In 1906, Bill Harley came up with a solution for that problem while he was still at school. It was basically a spring-type suspension system that absorbed the shock and handled rough surfaces smoothly. It would come to be known as the Springer front end, and the design stayed with the company for 40 years before it was replaced with telescopic forks. This new design was yet another example of the founders' dedication to innovation and improving the riding experience of their customers.

THE MOTOR COMPANY'S FIRST FORAY INTO RACING

By 1908, the Silent Grey Fellow had proven itself to be tough and reliable. The engine had grown to 26.8 cubic inches (440 cc), 4 horsepower, and a top speed of about 40 miles per hour. It was very popular with customers, and sales were robust. But it was heavy and slow, and the company advertising focused on its durability and reliability. It could hardly be considered a racing machine.

Motorcycle racing was becoming a very popular sport with both riders and spectators and was starting to influence buying decisions. Reluctant as they were to branch out into racing, the founders could not ignore the successes of their main competitors, Indian and Excelsior. The racing world was all about performance, and racing performance was selling a lot of motorcycles for Indian and Excelsior. If the Motor Company was going to keep pace, it would have to do something about becoming more visible in that world. There were already some private Harley owners doing well at endurance races where speed wasn't such a factor, and the company used that in their advertising every chance it got. But the founders realized that the company itself needed to step up to the plate.

They decided to enter an endurance race because speed wasn't a big factor, but toughness was. They chose one of the toughest and most respected—the Federation of American Motorcyclists (FAM) Endurance and Reliability Contest. It started in the Catskill Mountains in New York. Walter was the man to make the ride. Not only was he an avid race fan and a skilled rider, but he also had the grit to stick with any challenges the course might throw at him.

Walter Davidson with the 1908 Silent Grey Fellow that he rode to win the Federation of American Motorcyclists (FAM) Endurance Run in 1908. This photo was probably distributed to all the Harley dealers and used in advertising to emphasize the bike's performance as well as its durability and reliability. Courtesy of Harley-Davidson Archives. Copyright Harley-Davidson.

In June 1908, Walter joined 61 other riders for the first day of the race. He was the only one on a Harley. It was a grueling, 145-mile course from the Catskills to New York City over mountains, cow paths, rutted tracks, through water, and past a few surprises that the organizers threw in every year. It was a demanding course that called on a rider to reach down deep and pull everything he could from himself and his machine. Walter made the ride flawlessly, lost no points at the checkpoints, and finished the day with a perfect score. Fifteen other riders fell by the wayside.

Day two took the remaining 46 riders 180 miles around Long Island to Brooklyn. Again, Walter outdid the competition and won the Diamond Medal for the event with a perfect score of 1,000, plus an extra five points for his exceptional performance. A few days later, he won the fuel economy run and set an FAM record with an astonishing 188.234 miles per gallon.

Confidence or Outlaw Spirit?

Walter Davidson won the FAM Endurance and Reliability Contest in 1908 on a stock model Silent Grey Fellow. On top of that, unlike all the other riders, he carried no spare parts with him on the ride. He had faith in his machine and his own abilities. He had a bit of the outlaw in him, too.

Walter accomplished all of this on a factory-stock Silent Grey Fellow, with nothing special added for the race. It was the same bike sold to the public. In fact, he didn't even carry any spare parts with him. Now *that's* confidence! It didn't take long for word to get around about that tough, scrappy motorcycle and its extraordinary rider. Walter had definitely raised the bar on performance, and everyone took notice, especially the competition.

The following year, Walter and three other Harley riders won the team trophy for an endurance ride between Cleveland, Ohio, and Indianapolis, Indiana, again with a perfect score. Over the next few years, Walter also successfully rode an occasional endurance race to keep the company in the public eye and add to its growing performance record. Even though an official factory racing team wouldn't appear until 1914, the company had embraced the marketing value of racing. News of their own victories and those of private Harley owners became an established part of their advertising and marketing campaigns. The Motor Company was building an image—a brand. Can you hear the legend beginning to rumble?

ARTHUR THE DEALMAKER: MARKETING, ADVERTISING, AND DEALER NETWORKS

Arthur Davidson was a natural-born salesman. His enthusiasm about things he liked and believed in was contagious. Folks said Arthur could sell just about anything he was passionate about. And we know he was passionate about the motorcycles he and Bill Harley were building. Even as the first bikes were being built in 1903, Arthur got busy scouting other people to help sell them. In early 1904 C. H. Lang in Chicago, the very first Harley-Davidson dealer, sold one of those first three bikes.

Bicycle dealers were everywhere, so they were Arthur's first logical targets. They already had the showroom space and the salespeople, and a few were already selling motorcycles from their competitors. Given Arthur's magic touch, it didn't take much to convince them to add a few Harleys as well. Dealer recruitment began in earnest in 1907 as production at the factory was on the rise. He focused on areas with easy rail access for shipping the bikes to extend the company's reach as far as possible. As the dealership network began to grow, Arthur handled training for the salespeople, and he supplied dealers with advertising materials, mechanical specifications, and the latest news in bike development.

The only print media back then was newspapers, so Arthur put together an ad campaign that placed strategic newspaper ads in areas where dealerships were located. Photographs and handbills distributed to the dealers covered everything from the latest in motorcycle design to the performance of Harleys at the races. Arthur also supplied dealers with the company's first motorcycle catalogue to give out to customers. It was small—barely more than a brochure—but you can bet it got bigger fast in the coming years.

The main focus of their advertising was the same as the production focus—the strength and dependability of their machines. Still, they could not ignore the marketing power of racing performance. Before Walter took the plunge as an official factory rider in 1908 at the FAM, Harley racing victories had come from private owner/riders, the first one in 1905 in Chicago. And Harleys kept on winning for their private owners. Walter made the most of those victories in ads like this:

THE REAL TEST OF A MACHINE
Is in the Private Owner's Hands
And that is where the Harley-Davidson
MAKES GOOD EVERY TIME.[3]

Or this one that appeared a few years later in a motorcycle magazine:

No, we don't believe in racing and we don't make a practice of it, but when Harley-Davidson owners win races with their own stock machines hundreds of miles from the factory, we can't help crowing about it.[4]

The ads also spoke of freedom: freedom to go from place to place faster and easier, the freedom of the open road, and the freedom to move a little outside of the norm. They spoke of adventure and expressing individuality in a fun and carefree way. As the company built its image of strong, reliable motorcycles, it was also creating something more intangible, but just as powerful as the nuts and bolts. These were the first whispers of the Harley mystique.

Arthur's campaign worked and kept working. Orders for new bikes increased year after year, and nearly every year the factory size doubled. By the end of 1907, they had negotiated a contract to supply motorcycles for the Detroit Police Department with delivery in 1908. The first motorcycle cops rode Harleys.

Careful planning and meticulous execution of those plans were hallmarks of the company from its earliest days, whether it was building motorcycles or marketing. This kind of focus and clarity of purpose set

Harley-Davidson apart from all the others and was a key to the company's growing success. The founders were careful, they were calculating, they studied their customer base, and when they made a move, it was strategically planned to bring the maximum results. They knew that if they were to have a strong successful company, they needed a solid reputation that would endure. They got it and kept building on it.

After 1907 sales increased dramatically every year, sometimes tripling the previous year's sales. That trend continued until the early 1920s. But the best was yet to come. In 1908, Bill Harley finished school and returned to the company full-time. He wasted no time getting back to the drawing board, and the innovations he introduced to the line in the coming years would usher in the era of the big bikes. Exciting days in Harley history were on the way.

The Growing Years Timeline

1904   The Motor Company produced eight motorcycles, and the first dealership opened in Chicago, Illinois.

1905   Building began on a new factory on Juneau Avenue.

1906   Arthur and Walter left their day jobs to focus their attention fully on their growing company.

The company moved into the new factory, hired six more employees, and started producing about one motorcycle a week. Arthur put together the first catalogue, and the Silent Grey Fellow made its debut with a bigger engine and a new front-end suspension. The Springer front end would be the standard for the next 40 years.

1907   Factory size doubled and they hired on 18 more workers. Production tripled to 150 motorcycles.

William quit his job with the railroad early in the year and joined the company full-time.

The company became a corporation that year, with Walter as president, Bill the chief engineer and treasurer, Arthur the sales manager and secretary, and William vice president and works manager. The stock was divided evenly among them.

Arthur began recruiting dealers in earnest. He focused on bicycle dealers with showrooms and salespeople, and easy rail access for shipping to more distant locations. He began building his ad campaign at the same time, touting their bikes' strength, durability, and racing performance under private owner/riders.

1908 The company made its first official entry into racing when Walter entered and won the FAM Endurance Run with a perfect score. At the same time, he set an FAM record for fuel economy at 188.234 miles per gallon. As word of Walter's victory on the factory-stock Silent Grey Fellow spread, sales increased dramatically.

The Detroit Police Department took delivery of the first motorcycles for police duty, and traded in their horses for Harleys.

Bill Harley graduated from engineering school and returned to the company full-time late in the year.

NOTES

1. Harley-Davidson, Inc., *Harley-Davidson: Historical Overview 1903–1993* (Milwaukee, WI: Harley-Davidson, Inc., 1994), p. 17.

2. Jean Davidson, *Jean Davidson's Harley-Davidson Family Album* (Stillwater, MN: Voyageur Press, Inc., 2003), p. 29.

3. Tod Rafferty, *Harley-Davidson: The Ultimate Machine, 100th Anniversary Edition 1903–2003* (Philadelphia, PA: Courage Books, 2002), p. 15

4. Harley-Davidson, Inc., *Historical Overview 1903–1993* (Milwaukee, WI: Harley-Davidson, Inc., 1994), p. 22.

Chapter 5

The V-Twin Ushers in the Years of Innovation and Expansion, 1909–World War I

One of the first things Bill Harley did when he returned to the company in 1908 was beef up the Silent Grey Fellow. The engine size increased to give about 5-horsepower and a top speed of 50 miles per hour. The frame was strengthened and enlarged to handle the extra power and improve handling. Bill Harley had power on his mind, but he didn't want to tinker around too much with the single cylinder Silent Grey Fellow. It had an established reputation, a loyal following, and an expanding customer base. That was far too valuable to risk losing if increasing power meant compromising reliability. No, it would have to be a new bike altogether. The Silent Grey Fellow, with upgrades here and there, remained the workhorse for the company and stayed in production for 10 more years.

Bill was looking at something even more exciting—the v-twin engine. The v-twin was not unique to Harley-Davidson. In fact, the other major motorcycle manufacturers had been using it for a few years before Bill set his sights on it. Using two cylinders instead of one was the quickest and easiest way to nearly double power without adding a lot more weight. The V configuration fit nicely into a bicycle-type frame, so it didn't require a lot of chassis redesign. It was a natural for getting a more powerful motorcycle without a lot of hassle.

As he had done with the DeDion engine, Bill put his own design mark on the v-twin, and the first Harley with the new engine debuted in 1909, boasting 811 cc, 7 horsepower and a top speed of 60 miles per hour. Now that may not sound like such a big hot bike, but keep in mind that roads back then were still pretty primitive—still dirt, and muddy, rutted messes a lot of the time. 60 miles per hour was plenty fast for even the most adventurous spirit.

The factory produced 27 twins in 1909, but there were problems. The intake valve that worked well on the single engine proved unsuitable for the twin. The leather drive belt couldn't handle the increased power because it had no tensioning lever to modulate speed. That was odd because the tensioning lever was already standard on the single-engine models.

The Harley Sound Is Born

The distinctive Harley sound arrived with Bill Harley's version of the v-twin. Without getting too technical, it has to do with the way the pistons fire. In most engines, the pistons fire in a regular sequence so you get a sound sort of like "pop-pop-pop-pop-pop." Bill's design, however, fired in an irregular sequence with a pause so the sound is more like "pop-pop…pop-pop…pop-pop." Some people imitate it saying " potato-potato-potato-potato" real fast. Too bad this isn't an audio book!

In 1910, v-twin plans went back on the drawing board. Once the problems were solved, it was reintroduced in 1911. Among the changes was a new intake-exhaust system that became known as the F-head engine. It made both the v-twin and the single even more efficient and was standard on all Harleys until 1929.

Patents and Trademarks

The Bar and Shield Harley-Davidson logo appeared in 1910 and was trademarked in 1911. Bill Harley patented the Ful-Floteing seat in 1912. Even though they had "borrowed" and modified ideas from others in the past, they had not claimed them as their own. But they were very protective of their own innovations. From their earliest days, they made no bones about going after anyone who attempted to tread on their proprietary design territory. A 1911 ad in *Motorcycle Illustrated* proclaimed:

> The Harley-Davidson Ful-Floteing seat is *patented*. We have already been compelled to stop one manufacturer from using an infringing imitation, even after announcing a model incorporating a "spring seat post" as they called it.
>
> Any other infringement will be just as rigidly prosecuted and any dealers who make themselves liable by handling any machines that infringe on Harley-Davidson patents, will also be prosecuted to the full extent of the law.[a]

As the company grew, and innovation followed innovation, the company created an official Trademark Enforcement Division. Today, that division still stands watch over the company's products worldwide, and they don't cut anybody any slack now, either.

[a]Excerpt from a Harley-Davidson ad in *Motorcycle Illustrated,* November 30, 1911, from the collection of the Library of Congress. In the public domain.

Even more improvements came in 1912. A chain drive replaced the cantankerous leather belt, and the bikes were fitted with the first clutch ever on a motorcycle. It allowed riders to start the bike without pedaling and to stop or slow down without back-pedaling. It was a hit, especially with in-town riders stopping and starting in traffic. The engine grew to 1000 cc. Riders' rear ends got a welcome break, too, with the introduction of the "Ful-Floteing" spring-mounted, height-adjustable seat.

The new, improved v-twin was an immediate success. The single-cylinder Silent Grey Fellow soon got the chain drive, clutch, and more comfortable seat as well. By 1914, both models had both clutch and an honest-to-goodness brake pedal. In 1915 came the three-speed transmission and a rear passenger seat. A new battery and wiring system brought headlights for the first time. Prices went up too. The Silent Grey Fellow cost $290 (about $5,800 in today's dollars), and the v-twin went for $350 (about $7,000). The company had two solid machines that the buying public loved. By 1913, the company had sold nearly 13,000 motorcycles since its humble beginning in that backyard shed.

To meet the skyrocketing demand, the factory added space nearly every year. In 1912, construction began to expand the Juneau Avenue site

1915 Harley-Davidson v-twin with passenger seat, headlight, and squeeze-bulb horn. From the Collection of OnlyClassics.

into a huge, six-story complex that would serve as both factory and corporate headquarters. In 1909 they put out the first spare-parts catalogue for garages and do-it-yourself mechanics. The demand for parts increased so dramatically that machining, parts manufacturing, and accessories became a specialized department unto itself. The new building was designed with an area exclusively for parts and accessories production.

Harley Women in the 1910s

For as long as there have been Harleys, women, as well as men, have been riding them. Women were riding bicycles back then, weren't they? Why not motorcycles? There was no bad-boy, bad-girl image associated with motorcycles yet. Janet Davidson may well have been the first woman to ride a Harley, though nobody knows for sure. But don't you think that after she painted the tanks of the first bikes, she might have liked to cop a ride on one, too? Harley ads from as early as 1912 depict women on Harleys, and not just riding behind their men folk either. Many women took part in the same kinds of rides that men did, including long-distance endurance runs.

But none could touch Avis and Effie Hotchkiss, the first women to ride coast to coast on a motorcycle. In May 1915, the mother-daughter duo left Brooklyn, New York on a three-speed v-twin with a sidecar and headed for California. After a somewhat bumpy ride, they reached San Francisco in August. They turned right around and headed home taking an entirely different route, and arrived back in Brooklyn in October. They said they just wanted to see the country and have fun. And you can bet they did!

THE FIRST ACCESSORIES APPEAR

One of the foundational "bricks" laid by the founders from the very beginning was anticipating and meeting customer needs. They also knew it was important to keep the brand fresh in the public eye, so during the teen years, they began introducing accessories for the motorcycles. All of the founders, Bill and Arthur in particular, had a knack for knowing what might be the "next best thing" to put out, and they were usually right on the money. Like the v-twin, some were improvements on things already out there. However, the company had built such a reputation for quality that as soon as the Harley-Davidson name was attached to it, whatever it was would sell. Two of the most interesting new introductions were the forecar delivery van and the sidecar.

The 1913 forecar delivery van wasn't a van as we know it today. It was a three-wheel motorcycle with two wide-set wheels in front to support a large box-type container or basket. They were very popular in Europe, especially France, so Bill thought they just might fly in the United States as well. They were marketed to both commercial and recreational buyers, but got a lukewarm reception from the general public. Trying to steer two wheels in front on a rutted rural road while peering over a big box or basket seemed a bit much. Even though ads whimsically portrayed young men traveling with their ladies in the front basket for a lovely day in the country, the public didn't quite buy it. Businesses, however, were a different story. Flower shops, pharmacies, and other delivery-oriented businesses in towns and cities embraced them. The forecars weren't what you'd call a raging success, but commercial sales were steady enough to keep them in production for several years.

Sidecars came out in 1914 and were an unqualified success. They came in a few different sizes to accommodate the customer's needs—larger

Rural mail carrier with Harley and sidecar. Look at all those packages stacked on the mailboxes! Mail-order catalogues were getting to be the rage, and people could buy all sorts of things that were unavailable locally. Plus they didn't have to leave home to shop. The larger, heavy-duty sidecars were just the thing to handle the increasing volume of packages. Note how nicely padded and comfy that sidecar is, too. You can just imagine that mailman piling the wife and kids into it for a weekend outing. Courtesy of Harley-Davidson Archives. Copyright Harley-Davidson.

ones for delivery services, and smaller ones that would hold a couple of people for the family riders. They were easy to attach to the motorcycle and fairly easy to maneuver on all but the worst roads. Police departments and the postal service were the biggest customers when they first came out. By 1914 there were some 5,000 Harleys on the road with the postal service, and all of them added sidecars. A few years later, when the U.S. Military entered World War I, sidecar production went through the roof.

Sidecars also provided rich fodder for Arthur's marketing team to reach out to a whole new set of potential riders. Dealer handbills were full of pictures of sidecars with well-dressed families off for an outing together. Some of my favorite pictures, though, are those aimed at those who loved outdoor sports, like fishing. (I came across a wonderful one of two fellas on a Silent Grey Fellow, one driving, one riding on the passenger seat behind, and the sidecar brimming over with freshly caught fish. I doubt seriously, however, that the wife and kids would get near that smelly thing again after that.)

HARLEY TAKES THE OFFICIAL PLUNGE INTO RACING

Private Harley owners had been winning races for years before the company fielded its first factory racing team. The founders had been steadfastly resistant, saying their focus was on producing quality motorcycles for the general consumer and they weren't interested in getting into the racing business. However, the company didn't hesitate to capitalize on the victories of private owners in their advertising, and they were starting to appear a bit hypocritical. All of them enjoyed going to the races, too, especially Bill Harley.

Bill began to see that the faces in the crowds were getting younger and younger, and he saw potential new customers in those faces. They loved racing. Speed and high performance excited them. Bill recognized that the company would have to act on this emerging trend if it wanted to attract this new customer base. Both he and Walter also saw the value of racing as a testing ground for new design ideas. Bill was the one who finally lowered the boom and said, "let's go for it."

In 1913 Bill gave himself yet another title—Chief Racing Engineer—and hired engineer Bill Ottaway to be his assistant in the newly formed Racing Department. Ottaway had been the creative force behind the highly successful Thor racing team. They agreed to make only a few modifications to the factory stock bikes. They came up with a new gearbox, and worked on the v-twin to produce more power with less vibration and still hit 80 miles per hour. They made it plain from the beginning that any bike they produced for the racetrack must also be suitable for the street with only minor modifications.

THE RACING SCENE

In the early days there were four kinds of racing—road racing, cross-country racing, dirt track, and board track. Board track was, by far, the most exciting, the most popular, and the most dangerous. Races were run in what were known as motordromes—banked tracks made out of wood. That's right. The track itself was wood. The boards were laid edge to edge, just like a hardwood floor. They got dangerously slick from all the oil that leaked out of the bikes and if it rained on top of that, things got down-right treacherous. Crashes were common and so were serious injuries and fatalities. Back then, riders didn't have leathers and hard helmets. They basically wore heavy-duty versions of street clothes and close-fitting leather helmets, so there wasn't much there to protect them in a crash. As the tracks got bigger and the bikes got faster, the crashes got more spectacular, and more riders died. People started talking about "murder-dromes" and "murdercycles." A horrible crash in late 1912 at a New Jersey track that killed seven riders was pretty much the beginning of the end for board track racing. It took a few years, but one by one the major factories stopped sending out riders, and the craze faded away.

The dirt-track races were often run at the horse racing tracks with their deep, fine-powdered surfaces. The dust the bikes kicked up, especially flying through turns, meant the only guy who could really see where he was going was the one out front. As board track racing died out, many of those tracks were converted to dirt without the excessive dust.

Road racing and cross-country racing were a little less dangerous. They were also more attractive to amateur riders, especially cross-country. Many of the rallies sponsored by clubs and dealers were over the roads or the countryside and were open to riders of all stripes and experience. More experienced riders set their sights on cross-country endurance runs like the one Walter won in 1908.

HARLEY FIELDS ITS FIRST RACING TEAM

Bill Harley put together the first factory racing team in 1914. His first recruit was Leslie "Red" Parkhurst, a 6'4" redhead with a quick smile. Bill had seen him in a race at the Milwaukee motordrome board track and hired him on the spot. He spent the first year with Harley testing new racing machines. By 1915, Parkhurst was winning races for Harley-Davidson, including the 100-mile dirt track national in Saratoga, New York. In 1916, he won the two-mile board track national championship in Brooklyn, New York. 18,000 fans had turned out to watch the race in the new Sheepshead motordrome. It was the largest race crowd ever.

World War I brought a halt to racing, but Parkhurst was back on the team after it was over. In 1919 he won the biggest race of the year—the 200-mile road race in Marion, Indiana. He continued to ride for Harley until

1921, when he jumped ship for rival Excelsior. He was miserable there and soon returned to Milwaukee. By that time, he was married and had a family, so he raced only occasionally until he quit racing altogether in 1924.

Bill's second recruit was Otto Walker, who had been racing and winning as an amateur for several years on the West Coast. He joined the company race team shortly after Parkhurst but, because of injuries received in a crash, didn't see any action until 1915. That year he brought Harley-Davidson its first national victory in the 300-mile Venice, California road race. He topped that win with another a few months later at the Dodge City 300, the biggest racing event in the country. He won both on factory-stock Harleys. The company's sales jumped dramatically after those two victories.

By the end of the decade, others had joined the team, including Ralph Hepburn, Ray Weishaar, Albert "Shrimp" Burns, Maldwyn Jones, and Fred Ludlow. Hepburn made his mark shortly after joining in 1919 when he won the prestigious 200 Mile National Championship at Ascot Park in Los Angeles. Harley racing was on its way, and it wasn't long before the team became known as the Wrecking Crew as they demolished the competition.

Harley Team Racing in the 1910s

1915   Red Parkhurst won the 100-mile dirt track national in Saratoga, New York.

Otto Walker won the national road racing championship at the 300-mile Venice, California road race.

Walker won the Dodge City 300, the most prestigious motorcycle racing event in the country.

1916   Parkhurst won the 100-mile FAM board track championship in Brooklyn, New York.

1919   Parkhurst won the 200-mile Marion, Indiana road race. Ralph Hepburn took second, Otto Walker third.

Otto Walker won the board track championship in Brooklyn, New York.

MARKETING HITS FEVER PITCH, DEALERSHIPS MULTIPLY AND OVERSEAS MARKETS OPEN UP

Arthur's sales and dealer recruiting team had been growing as fast the rest of the company, and they'd been busy. By 1912, there were over 200 dealerships and counting in the United States. The company had also scored more large-scale contracts to supply motorcycles to police departments, the military, and commercial fleets that provided delivery and courier services.

The lion's share of credit for the phenomenal yearly sales growth belonged to Arthur's aggressive, well-organized marketing campaign. By 1912, a couple of motorcycle magazines had popped onto the scene, extending the advertising reach beyond newspapers and dealer hand-bills. Arthur's team took full advantage of them with full page ads, and sometimes double page ads, proclaiming the newest models, the latest innovations, and the successes of private Harley owners at the races. Ads touted "the motorcycle with the Ful-Floteing seat" in 1912, the 6-horse-power singles and the 3-speed twins in 1914. They had something new and exciting every year that the competition didn't. They were also the only manufacturer to guarantee the horsepower of their machines.

Before the company officially fielded a factory race team, they used the victories of private owners to their advantage. Two 1912 models took first and second at the Kansas State Championships on a course through mud and muck and slushy snow. The winning rider broke the old records on a Silent Grey Fellow right out of the crate. A double page ad in *Motorcycle Illustrated* said:

> the road test given the Harley-Davidson at the factory is a *real* road test, which makes unnecessary any further adjustments or tinkering on the part of the dealer or rider. Harley-Davidson motorcycles are not in the same class with any other motorcycle on the 1912 market today.
>   . . . the close finish of these two machines is only a sample of the consistent performances that have become a habit with the sturdy "Silent Grey Fellow."[1]

Another 1912 ad in *Motorcycling* made hay of the speed of a private Harley owner's 8-horsepower twin as he won a big California road race, hitting 68 miles per hour:

> Harley-Davidsons are not racing machines, but because they are designed right and built right, they will outrun any stock machine of equal horsepower or piston displacement.[2]

The company also used the ads to take a few jabs at the competition. In this 1911 *Motorcycle Illustrated* ad introducing the new Harley model, they didn't mince words.

> Just put yourself in the place of our competitors when they saw our announcement. . . . Here was the new Harley-Davidson with the Ful-Floteing Seat and Free Wheel Control, at the same price they were figuring on getting in 1912 for an out-of-date type of

machine with a rigid seat and a dinky little makeshift clutch of the "slip 'em in easy" or "grab" variety stuck on to the engine or countershaft as an afterthought. What would you do? The only thing they could do was cut their price below that of a new Harley-Davidson, thereby admitting, as they admitted, that their machine was an obsolete model?

. . . By one stroke, all rigid seat motorcycles, all spring frame models and all engine or countershaft clutches were made obsolete.[3]

Ouch!

The company made clever use of ads to recruit new dealers, too. Full page ads featured dealers that were successful, heaping praise on their accomplishments and sales figures against competitors. On the one hand, the ads acknowledged that the competitors' products were good. With the other hand, they pointed out that these competitors were at a disadvantage because they didn't have the company selling system. They didn't say what that system was but enticed new dealers by saying that it was "a system that has increased the average Harley-Davidson dealer's business by 82½% this year. A system that will do as much for you."[4] Intriguing, isn't it? And it was incredibly effective in adding new dealers every year.

Magazines had become such valuable and successful tools for spreading the word about Harley that the company launched its own magazine, *The Enthusiast*, in 1916. Each issue had the latest news from the factory, from the racetracks, and from owners, and readership was brisk. The magazine has helped sell a lot of Harleys over the years, and is still being published today—the longest reign for a motorcycle magazine in the world.

What about Cars?

As you recall, Henry Ford came out with the Model A Ford automobile in 1903—the same year as the first Harley. The Model T came out in 1908 and would become enormously popular. That year, the price for a Model T was $850, about three times more than a Harley with a sidecar. As Ford's assembly line process was perfected, the price dropped to $550 in 1913, and to $440 in 1915. Still a little more expensive than a motorcycle, but getting closer. Harley-Davidson's sales were leveling out from the earlier years, and Ford's installment buying plan meant more people were buying cars. The threat to the motorcycle market was getting more substantial. Then came World War I, and the playing field changed dramatically in Harley-Davidson's favor. The military needed motorcycles, not cars.

U.S. sales were solid—about 5,000 motorcycles a year—so the company started eyeing markets overseas. Their first customer was Japan, and the first Harleys shipped out in 1912. In 1913, the company joined up with an international distributor in London to begin sales throughout Europe. Shipments had barely begun when World War I broke out, and everything was put on hold. But those first Harleys were enormously popular, so the stage was set for vigorous international dealer expansion after the war.

HARLEY GOES TO WAR

Even before the United States entered World War I in 1917, the military was buying Harleys. General John J. "Black Jack" Pershing and his troops had been playing cat and mouse with Mexican general Pancho Villa after he began attacking small border towns in the United States in 1916. He eluded them at every turn—riding an Indian motorcycle—and the hunt was abandoned when the United States joined the war effort.

Just before the United States entered the war, Harley began shipping motorcycles to supply the European market. The British military had commandeered all the motorcycles for the war effort, and the motorcycle companies turned their production to the weapons of war. That left civilians with no source for new machines. Harley seized the opportunity to fill the gap. Business was fairly brisk considering the circumstances, and Harley's reputation for solid, reliable machines began to spread.

In 1917 the military bought about one-third of the motorcycles Harley manufactured that year. The company was careful not to commit its entire

WWI Harley with sidecar at battalion headquarters. From the collection of OnlyClassics.

production so it could still meet the demands of the market at home and its smaller overseas market. The next year, it committed half of its production to military sales. By the end of the war, the military had bought nearly 20,000 motorcycles, most of them Harleys. The company produced one workhorse model for the war—the 1,000 cc "J" 61 F-head. Most of the machines were fitted with sidecars, some with gun mounts. They served as couriers, transport for supplies and ammunition, and vehicles for transporting wounded soldiers from battlefields to field hospitals. They also toted their fair share of officers and attachés from place to place quickly.

Harley-Davidson as a company supported the war effort at home as well. The tone of its ads changed to more patriotic themes, and *The Enthusiast* ran articles keeping everyone up on the war effort and Harley's role in it. It encouraged mechanics to bone up on motorcycle maintenance in case they were called up to serve. Early on, the company opened a new department called the Quartermasters School to train military motorcycle mechanics. After the war, that department became the company Service School and shifted to factory training civilian Harley-Davidson mechanics.

Indian Provides an Opening

Indian also supplied motorcycles to the military and shifted all their production to meet that need, virtually abandoning their domestic market. It was largely an economic move, but it proved to be a near-disastrous decision for them for two reasons.

1. Indian was in rough financial shape when the war broke out and lowered their prices for the military hoping to attract a large contract.[a] Bill Harley and Walter Davidson had negotiated much more lucrative contracts and ended up selling more motorcycles at a higher price than Indian did.
2. When Indian left their dealers at home hanging with few bikes to sell, Arthur and his recruiting team went to work to bring them into the Harley-Davidson fold. After the war, Indian discovered their dealer network significantly reduced.[b]

This was a classic example of the meticulous way the founders worked their business. They planned carefully, carried through on those plans flawlessly, and seized every opportunity to expand their market.

[a]William Green, *Harley-Davidson: The Living Legend* (New York: Crescent Books, 1993), 17.
[b]Martin Norris, *Rolling Thunder* (Philadelphia, PA: Courage Books, 1992), 14.

On November 11, 1918, the war officially ended, and the day after the Armistice was signed, one of the greatest photo ops a company could ask for occurred. American Corporal Roy Holtz of Chippewa Falls, Wisconsin was the first American to enter Germany after the war. He rode in on a beat-up, shell-shocked Harley with a battered sidecar and the headlight shot out. That photo ran in newspapers and magazines all over the world, and don't think for one minute that Arthur's marketing team didn't use it to the max.

The company made the transition back to civilian production smoothly and easily. It had learned a few new tricks during those years that improved the processes and machining techniques that served it well in coming years. It had also made a very smart move in 1917 when it began producing bicycles to fill the gap in lowered domestic motorcycle production. It outsourced production to the Davis Sewing Machine Company in Ohio, while the dealer networks handled sales, and the venture was profitable enough to continue for several more years.

The company had successfully met its commitments to the war effort while remaining loyal to its customers at home. After the war, its sales began to climb again, and overseas dealer recruitment hit high gear. By the time 1920 rolled around, Harley-Davidson was the largest motorcycle maker in the world, with over 2,000 dealers in 67 countries. Why? Because the founders had stuck to the principles upon which the company was founded: build a great product, listen to your customers and keep them happy, keep new customers coming, make the best use of resources and manpower, and make plans carefully and strategically. They kept their eyes open for every new opportunity to expand their customer base both in the United States and abroad. They held their original vision and kept the brand image vibrant in the public eye. They were a team that didn't waver, and that steadfastness would carry the company successfully through the dark days ahead.

You Decide

Now you get to sit in on a planning and strategy session as the founders work on an idea for a new motorcycle to add to their line in 1919. Take a few minutes to think about it, about how far the company has come and what it has become in the minds and hearts of its customers. Then you decide how you would proceed and what you think the outcome might be. Once you're through, turn the page to see what the company decided and how it turned out. No peeking.

The war is over, domestic sales are doing well, more dealers have joined the Harley family, and overseas markets are expanding by leaps and bounds. The v-twin is an unqualified success and a strong part of the Harley-Davidson image. Now that we've dropped the single-cylinder Silent Grey Fellow, maybe it's time to add something new.

We've been looking at a new twin-cylinder engine put out in Britain with cylinders that lie flat rather than vertical like the v-twin. It might fly here as well. There's less vibration and it's quieter. Some of our customers have said the vibration at higher speeds is annoying and others have commented about the v-twins being somewhat loud.

What if we built a bike with that cylinder alignment instead of the V configuration? We could focus our marketing on the smoother, quieter ride and how much easier it is to work on than the v-twin. It would be a middleweight engine—not quite 600 cc—with a top speed of 45 miles per hour. That might really appeal to a lot of people who aren't interested in speed, but are more interested in comfort—more of a gentleman's motorcycle. Mechanics would appreciate the easier accessibility to the engine for maintenance, too.

The Model T has also started to cut into our market, and we only have to look at Indian to see how sales of their big bikes are suffering. We could offer this new bike at a lower price than the Model T and appeal to a more budget-conscious sector of the market. Since the British version is selling well in Europe, it would give our dealers over there the Harley version to add to their line-ups.

OK, now let's play devil's advocate. Changing the engine configuration will require some alterations in machining and production processes. We made that shift quickly and easily when we geared up for war production, so it shouldn't be much of a problem. But the new engine configuration could require changes in the chassis, and we might be looking at some serious do-over there.

If we're going to introduce a new model, shouldn't we stick with what we know works and consider making a 600 cc v-twin instead of a whole new engine configuration? It certainly would be just as powerful and fast as the British model. Are we certain that the vibration and noise are big enough issues with enough of our customers to justify a whole new engine style? We could offer it at about the same price as this new one, maybe even less because we wouldn't have to change production methods. Will we be able to lure the "gentlemen" away from the Model-T with a motorcycle whose biggest claim to fame is a quiet, smooth ride?

And, finally, it's important to maintain our strong brand image. Customers really identify with the v-twin, and a totally new engine might be too much of a change for them to swallow. That's very important here in the United States. Even if the European market embraces it, we need to stay strong in our primary market here at home.

Now you decide.

"You Decide" Answer: The 1919 Sport Twin

The company decided to build the bike. It was a fairly snazzy little number with a more vibrant green color than the drab Army green that was standard on all Harleys after the war. It was a quiet, smooth, but somewhat boring ride. It flopped in the United States but sold well overseas. The lower price tag didn't seem to matter. Americans had come to the point that if they wanted cheaper transportation, they bought a Ford. People who bought motorcycles wanted performance and that meant the v-twin.

Unfortunately for Harley, that same year, Indian introduced the 600 cc v-twin Scout. It was more powerful than the Sport Twin, but the biggest factor in its success was that it *was* a v-twin. In fact, many people in the industry were shocked that Harley would deviate from the engine that had become the symbol of the American motorcycle.

Harley continued to produce the Sport Twin until 1923, mostly for the overseas market. And Harley learned a good lesson. Had they stuck with the v-twin and put out a 600 cc model, their huge brand status and loyal following would probably have made it a smashing success. From that point on, the company stuck with what worked, and built on it.

What the company did *not* do was consider it a failure, any more than Bill and Arthur considered their first bike a failure when it couldn't make it up hills on its own. They took it as a good lesson, banked the money from European sales, and let it fan the flames of future innovation.

Years of Innovation and Expansion Timeline

1909   Harley-Davidson put out its first v-twin powered motorcycle.

1910   The company used the "Bar and Shield" logo for the first time, and trademarked it a year later.

Privately owned Harleys began to make a big mark in the racing scene.

1911   The new and improved v-twin reappeared and was a success. The new F-head engine becomes standard on all Harleys until 1929. Other improvements included a chain drive, clutch, and the more comfortable Ful-Floteing seat.

1912 There were 200 Harley dealers nationwide, and the first sales outside the United States began with shipments to Japan.

Construction began on a new six-story factory/corporate headquarters building on the Juneau Avenue site.

The company put out its first spare parts catalogue and set up a new department just for parts and accessories.

1913 The company finally decided that a racing team would be to its advantage, so Bill Harley formed the Racing Department with William Ottaway as his assistant.

By the end of the year, they had sold nearly 13,000 motor-cycles.

The Forecar Delivery Van entered service for commercial markets.

1914 The company fielded its first racing team, which wasted no time in dominating the sport and picking up the nickname "The Wrecking Crew."

F-head singles and v-twins got new clutch and brake pedals, as well as headlights.

Sidecars made their successful debut.

1915 Harley motorcycles got 3-speed transmissions and a passen-ger seat.

Avis and Effie Hotchkiss were the first women to ride coast to coast on a motorcycle.

1916 The company began publishing *The Enthusiast* magazine, which is still in publication today.

Sales were solid—about 5,000 motorcycles a year.

1917 The company geared up to produce motorcycles and sidecars for the military during World War I. About one-third of that year's production was sold for the war effort.

The company opened the Quartermasters School to train military mechanics to work on motorcycles. The school con-verted to training civilian mechanics after the war.

Harley-Davidson bicycles hit the market for the first time.

1918 Half of the company's production was sold to the military.

NOTES

1. Excerpt from a Harley-Davidson ad in *Motorcycle Illustrated*, December 14, 1911, from the collection of the Library of Congress. In the public domain.

2. Excerpt from a Harley-Davidson ad in *Motorcycling*, December 12, 1912, from the collection of the Library of Congress. In the public domain.

3. Excerpt from a Harley-Davidson ad in *Motorcycle Illustrated*, November 30, 1911, from the collection of the Library of Congress. In the public domain.

4. Excerpt from a Harley-Davidson ad in *Motorcycle Illustrated*, September 11, 1911, from the collection of the Library of Congress. In the public domain.

Chapter 6

The Roaring Twenties

Harley-Davidson greeted the twenties sitting in the catbird seat. They were selling more motorcycles than anyone else in the world, they had an enormous 6-story facility with nearly 2,000 employees, and an advertising budget of $250,000 a year (nearly $3 million in today's dollars). *The Enthusiast* had tens of thousands of subscribers around the world. People came from far and wide to tour the factory where the awesome Harley-Davidson motorcycle was made. Times were good. But not for long.

People had started buying cars—millions of them. Henry Ford's mass production assembly lines made a new Model T as affordable as a new Harley with a sidecar. Once other carmakers adopted assembly lines, there were cars everywhere. In 1910, there were 500,000 cars on the road. By 1920, 8 million.

In 1920, Harley-Davidson sold over 28,000 motorcycles, many of them models left over from the war production that proved to be very popular. Then things started to slip. In 1921, sales fell to a little over 10,000, the lowest in 10 years. For the first time in its history, the company posted a loss for the year. After a "family council" of founders and employees, the company shut down for a month, cut wages, and back-burnered the racing team to save money.

Harley-Davidson Hired Women from the Get-Go

Even in the early days, Harley-Davidson was an equal opportunity employer. Sort of. They hired women for both office jobs and jobs on the shop floor. However, they would only hire unmarried women with the understanding that once they married, the job was history. Like most people in those days, the founders felt that a woman's first priority was raising a family and tending the home.

Nobody sat around wringing their hands during the down time. They used the time to evaluate their position, and come up with some new strategies to survive. They had seen many of the existing 200 motorcycle makers go down the tubes quickly, and they had no intention of joining them. You can just imagine Bill at his drafting table working on new design possibilities. Or Arthur huddling with his dealers and salespeople to brainstorm new ad campaigns and sales strategies. Or William consulting employee leaders for their input on ways to cut production costs without compromising quality. Or frugal Walter going over every detail of the financial ledgers to see what could be shaved without sacrificing manpower or product integrity. Over the next couple of years, they made several strategic moves to keep the company going, keep people working, and keep producing motorcycles that people would buy in spite of the new fascination with cars.

STRATEGIC MOVE 1—TALK TO THE COMPETITION

In early 1922, the company made the unprecedented move of sitting down with its main competitor, Indian, to work out a deal to present a united front against the threat of the automobile. They agreed hold the line on their pricing. No price wars, no undercutting. It was a good first step. Now, some might call that price-fixing, and maybe it was, but it helped both companies stay afloat in tough financial times.[1] A short time later, Harley introduced a bigger version of the "J" model that had served them so well since the war. The 18-horsepower, 1200 cc 74 v-twin was a head-to-head competitor with Indian's Big Chief. Even though the price was the same, and they were essentially sticking to their agreement, the move raised a few eyebrows. It was a hit, and most certainly let the world know that the Harley/Indian rivalry was still alive and well.

Harley Team Racing in the 1920s

1920   Red Parkhurst broke 23 speed records.

Otto Walker won the 100-mile national road race at Ascot Park, California.

Harley rented the Sheepshead board track in Brooklyn, New York, to try for a 24-hour solo record. Parkhurst set a new record of 1,452 miles in less than 24 hours after sitting out a couple of hours because of hard rain. You can bet that board track was slick as glass after that.

1921   Otto Walker set a new speed record for motorcycle racing of over 100 miles per hour on a board track in California.

Ralph Hepburn won the Dodge City 300 road race. Since it was the last running of that race, every factory team in the country had their best riders there.

1922   Harley racers took all at the National Championships.

1925   Joe Petrali joined the Harley team.

STRATEGIC MOVE 2—SUSPEND THE RACING BUDGET FOR A WHILE

When sales plunged, the company decided to cut expenses by devoting all its production dollars to civilian sales, not factory adaptations for racing. For a while, the factory racing team had kept going with what it had, winning races left and right and setting records, even through the worst of times. Though down to skin and bones, the Wrecking Crew never quite disappeared. Most of the factory race bikes were sold to European racers, and a few of the Harley factory riders headed to Europe to continue their winning ways.

How Harleys Became Hogs

In the early 1920s, the Harley-Davidson factory race team had a small pig for the team mascot. After each of his victories, Red Parkhurst would carry the pig with him on the victory lap. It didn't take long for the nickname "hog" to stick.

STRATEGIC MOVE 3—BEEF UP INTERNATIONAL SALES

Even though sales at home were suffering, international sales were steady and helped keep the company afloat. The British and European motorcycle industries were still reeling from the war, and Harley stepped in to fill the gap. The company also had its sights set on newer, untapped markets. Enter Englishman Alfred Rich Child. Arthur had hired him a few years earlier, and he had proven himself a skillful salesman, successfully setting up new dealerships in the United States, Canada, and Europe. This time his assignments were Africa and the Far East—Japan, Korea, China, and Manchuria.

He set sail for Cape Town, South Africa, with a Model J and sidecar in late 1921. His goal? Ride from Cape Town the full length of Africa to Cairo, Egypt, sell motorcycles and set up dealerships along the way. He did it, too, even though there were spots where he and his bike had to be carried by native porters through impassable jungle and over rivers without bridges. By the time he rumbled into Cairo, he had taken paid orders for about 400 motorcycles and started quite a few new dealerships.[2]

Child barely had time to unpack his steamer trunk back home before he was sent to Asia. The company had been exporting motorcycles and setting up dealerships in Japan since 1912, but the network had fallen into disarray, not to mention some shady dealings. It presented a huge challenge that needed to be solved quickly because Indian had established a firm, successful market there. Things were such a mess when Child arrived that he fired all the distributors except one—the Koto Trading Company.

Koto was a little dodgy itself, selling "bootleg" Harleys originally destined for other places. But the key word was "selling," and they were selling them well. In 1924, with Harley-Davidson's blessing, Child set up the Harley-Davidson Motorcycle Sales Company of Japan with Koto in Tokyo and installed himself as managing director. Sales of motorcycles and spare parts took off quickly, and within two years, Indian was eating their dust. Child also negotiated big contracts with the military because Harleys were the only heavyweights imported at the time that were designed and built for hard, demanding work.

Back in Milwaukee, Harley came out with a 350 cc single-cylinder model in 1926 in response to the European demand for a lighter weight racing bike. It became known as the Peashooter because of its rapid pop-pop-pop sound. It had no brakes, clutch, or transmission and could hit 100 miles an hour. The Peashooter enjoyed great success at the tracks in Europe and Australia and, later on, in the United States. The street version sold very well in Europe, and fairly well in the United States, largely because of its racing reputation.

STRATEGIC MOVE 4—STICK WITH WHAT WORKS

After the somewhat disappointing experience with the Sport Twin in 1919, the founders decided not to fiddle around too much with the trusty and popular v-twin. The 1000 cc "J" 61 model had helped power Harley-Davidson to the top of the heap, and it proved to be a mainstay during the early 1920s. It became the foundation bike. Other than the "74," launched in 1922 to match Indian's Big Chief, there would be no major model changes or new introductions for the domestic market till the end of the decade. The company did, however, replace the rectangular gas tank with a teardrop shape. It was a sleeker look, and became a distinctly Harley look from then on.

STRATEGIC MOVE 5—REVAMP AND RAMP
UP THE AD CAMPAIGN

Arthur's fat advertising budget didn't escape the axe either. But at the same time, he needed to keep Harley in the public eye and attract new customers. He and his clever band of ad wizards came up with a multifaceted approach—a little of the tried-and-true, a couple of new twists, and something more indefinable. More than just nurturing a brand image, they began to build the first glimmers of the Harley-Davidson mystique.

Shipments of motorcycles and sidecars to dealers around the country and Canada rode the rails. Big banners stretching the length of rail cars proclaimed a "solid carload of Harley-Davidson motorcycles & sidecars." It was clever, cheap, easy publicity that got attention in every town and rural byway those trains passed through.

Ads continued to trade on Harley's reliability and durability but, after the strategic meeting with Indian, took fewer potshots at the competition. The Wrecking Crew's successes provided more than enough exciting ad copy. Owner-ridden Harleys were winning big on the international circuits, as well, both on the tracks and in grueling endurance races. While the ads crowed about the victories, the big message was that these victories were just one more example of Harley's superior build and performance. A 1922 ad touted the success of an Australian owner on a factory Harley with 10,000 miles on it, as he and his sidecar passenger broke the record for the 580-mile Adelaide-to-Melbourne endurance run.

> And during the entire trip not a tool had to be touched or an adjustment made.
> This performance emphasizes the sterling qualities of Harley-Davidson. In every part of the world, Harley-Davidson is continually demonstrating through unmatchable feats that it is without equal.[3]

Harley-Davidson's First Finance Company

Henry Ford's installment buying plans for Model Ts had helped get a lot of folks behind the wheel, and, eventually, all the carmakers picked up on it. It was a huge factor in the rapid growth of the automobile industry. Taking a cue from that success, Arthur recruited other investors to start the Kilbourn Finance Corporation in 1923 to allow new customers to buy motorcycles on credit. Arthur served as president, and the move helped tremendously to boost sagging sales.

Sidecars got a marketing push, with ads encouraging them as add-ons for passengers as a more economical, reliable, and fun way to travel than a car. Bill Harley and Walter Davidson even started appearing in the ads inviting people to give their motorcycle/sidecar combos a test drive.

Commercial ads began to focus on utility and cost-savings, saying that motorcycles with sidecars and the forecar delivery vans were much more economical than automobiles for small deliveries. "Don't use tonnage truck for poundage delivery. Use a Harley-Davidson," one ad advised. Other ads encouraged gas and electric companies to use motorcycles rather than cars for their meter readers. It all worked. Sidecar and forecar delivery van sales hit an all-time high in the 1920s.

Other accessories got more attention, too. For those who didn't want to invest in a sidecar, but still wanted to accommodate a passenger, an extra seat and an extra set of handlebars on the back could be installed for a few extra dollars. Chains for the rear tires were added to make going in the snow a breeze. And no self-respecting rider should be caught dead in clothing other than Harley's own line of riding togs, offered exclusively through its dealers. Clothing had been available through dealers for a while, but when every penny counted, it paid to make potential customers more aware of the range of available products and options.

Commercial accounts had been the backbone of the company's revenues all along. Speeding cars and rum runners during prohibition meant police departments needed more motorcycles to apprehend the perps, and Harleys were the machines of choice. In 1926, the company formed a separate department exclusively for police sales.

The U.S. Postal Service upped its orders of bikes and sidecars to cover the additional routes that came with rural population growth. The military also kept some contracts going for training and police work, and kept sending their mechanics to the company's service school.

Arthur's team also began to focus on a new emerging market—women. Of course, we already know that women were riding Harleys long before the 1920s, but they had not been considered a force in the market. However, after women won the right to vote in 1920, there was a more independent and rebellious spirit to appeal to in the ads. In 1921, ads appeared with photos of well-dressed women riders, with headlines like "the feature refined, woman-kind Harley-Davidson." They focused on the joys of riding in the great outdoors, and compared riding a motorcycle to riding horses in earlier days as a perfectly respectable pastime. Publicity photos of women riders with their men folk in sidecars made the rounds of magazine ads and dealer handouts. And you can bet that the ads also had a plug for the lovely split riding skirts only available at Harley-Davidson dealers. Sales to women did increase, but they didn't become a market force until many years later.

The ads also began to play a more intangible tune that spoke more to the spirit of riding than its utility. A new, more mystical layer began to settle over the brand image that added even more power to the Harley-Davidson name. Headlines like "all roads lead to joyland," and "the sport of a thousand joys" were accompanied by photos of riders weaving through narrow woodland paths or along the shores of a lake or stream—places you couldn't go with a car. Some ads showed a rider with a passenger in a sidecar (usually a beautiful woman), off for some remote adventure inaccessible by car. One of the most powerful headlines of the 1920s was "get a kick out of life," and it appeared over and over and over for several years. None of these ads had anything to do with durability or reliability or winning races. They had to do with adventure and individuality and being a free spirit to go wherever the notion led you. They had to do with being a bit of an outlaw.

THE LIGHT AT THE END OF THE TUNNEL

The comprehensive, full-court press by the Harley team paid off. Sales slowly began to improve and by 1929 hit the highest level since

Harley Women—1920s

Bessie Stringfield, shown here in later years with her 1950s Harley Panhead, was known as the Motorcycle Queen of Miami and started riding motorcycles when she was 16. In the late 1920s, she became the first African American woman to ride solo across the country. In the 1930s and 1940s, she toured all 48 states, Europe, Brazil, and Haiti. When World War II broke out, she signed on as an Army motorcycle courier and carried classified documents back and forth across the country in her saddlebags.

She took part in hill climbs and did stunt riding at carnivals to pick up extra cash. She once won a dirt track race disguised as a man, but her victory evaporated as soon as she took off her helmet. Women weren't allowed on the tracks then.

She settled in Miami and founded the Iron Horse Motorcycle Club. She owned 27 Harleys during her lifetime. At one point, her doctor told her to quit riding because of a heart condition. She refused, saying, "If I don't ride, I won't live long. And so I never quit." She kept on riding almost up until her death in 1993 at age 82.

In 2000 the American Motorcyclist Association created an award in her name to recognize women in the sport of motorcycling. She was inducted into the Motorcycle Hall of Fame in 2002.

Bessie Stringfield, shown here in later years with her 1950s Harley Panhead. From the author's private collection.

1919. Even though they weren't up to the full power they once enjoyed, Harley-Davidson had fared better than most motorcycle makers. By the end of the decade, very few were left standing. Indian and Excelsior were the company's only real competition, and Excelsior was on shaky ground.

Other than the 1926 Peashooter, no new models were introduced until 1928. The Peashooter had been a response to a specific demand, not a speculative move by the company, so it was a fairly safe bet. But that didn't mean that Bill Harley's design team had been idle. Quite the contrary. When the timing was right, they brought out some new upgrades to the trusty J model. The twin cam JD 74 (1200 cc) came out in 1928. Twin cams meant a more efficient engine that was easier to tune, higher horsepower, and a top speed near 100 miles per hour. The JD 74 was the most expensive in the Harley line at $370 (about $4,400 today). The 1000 cc and 1200 cc models got quieter mufflers and all the new models featured front brakes for the first time.

Motorcycle Engines 101—What the Heck Is a Twin Cam?

The cam is the heart of a 4-cycle engine like the Harley-Davidson. The v-twin engine has two cylinders, each with two valves—one for air intake, one for exhaust. Simply put, a cam is a round gear with knobs on it that turns round and round. As it turns, it pushes up a little rod that opens the valve to let fresh air into the cylinders to mix with gasoline from the carburetor. The resulting air/gasoline mist ignites from a spark from the spark plug. This gives the engine the power to go. The cam also opens the exhaust valve to release the gases from the "explosion." The whole process literally happens in a nanosecond. In the early days, only one cam worked the valves on both cylinders. The twin cam engine gave a cam to each cylinder, greatly improving engine function and efficiency.

In 1929, the D 45 (750 cc) model came out to challenge similar models by Indian and Excelsior. It had its problems, though, and ended up costing the company and its dealers a bundle before all the bugs were worked out. It had 2 headlights and an ear-blaster horn. The headlights didn't get anybody too excited and were dropped the next year. The model morphed over the years into the WL, and it became one of Harley's most popular and reliable engines, known later as the Flathead, and was still in production until 1973. The company also introduced the 1200 cc VL in 1929. It was a heavyweight bike known for its easy maintenance aimed at the police market.

The D 45—An Ironic Twist of Fate

While Bill Harley and his team were ironing out the initial troublesome kinks of the D 45, Excelsior came out with a similar model called the Super X. Arthur Constantine, who had left Harley under less than happy circumstances in 1925, designed it. He went to work for Excelsior shortly thereafter with the design still in his head. The Super X sold well, and helped keep floundering Excelsior's head above water for a little while longer.

Things were definitely looking up in 1929. Harley turned out about 22,000 bikes, and the overseas markets were growing. Then came the crash. In October of that year, the stock market fell to pieces. The light at the end of the tunnel turned out to be a high-speed train called the Great Depression.

Roaring Twenties Timeline

1920   Harley-Davidson was the largest motorcycle company in the world, with dealers in 67 countries.

Harleys became known as "hogs" after winning factory racers carried their pig mascot on each victory lap.

1921   As more people bought cars, Harley sales plunged to the lowest point in 10 years. To cut costs, the factory closed down for a month, cut wages, and put the racing team on hold. Many factory race bikes were sold to European riders and some Harley riders headed overseas as well.

Alfred Rich Child rode the full length of Africa on a model J with sidecar to sell motorcycles and set up new dealerships.

Advertising began to target women as a new market. Advertising also began to play on the more indefinable qualities of freedom, individuality, and adventure.

1922   Harley-Davidson founders sat down with the management at rival Indian for the first of many price management meetings to keep prices steady in the face of a common enemy—the automobile.

Harley rolled out the 1000 cc v-twin 74 to rival Indian's Big Chief.

1923   Arthur Davidson and a group of investors established the Kilbourn Finance Corporation to allow customers to buy Harleys on credit.

1924   Alfred Rich Child set up the Harley-Davidson Motorcycle Sales Company of Japan with the Koto company in Tokyo, and began importing motorcycles and spare parts.

1925   Teardrop shape gas tanks replaced the old rectangular standards.

1926   Harley produced the 350 cc Peashooter in response to overseas market demands for a lighter racing bike. Both the racing version and a later street version enjoyed robust sales in Europe and eventually in the United States.

The company formed a separate department dedicated to police sales.

1927   Bessie Stringfield became the first African American woman to cross the United States on a motorcycle.

1928   Harley introduced the twin cam, 1200 cc JD 74 with a top speed of 100 miles per hour.

1000 cc and 1200 cc bikes got quieter mufflers, and all new models had front brakes for the first time.

1929   The 750 cc D 45 appeared on the scene, with 2 headlights and a fearsome horn. It would become known as the Flathead, one of Harley's most popular and reliable engines.

The stock market crashed in October, setting the stage for the Great Depression.

NOTES

    1. William Green, *Harley-Davidson: The Living Legend* (New York: Crescent Books, 1993), 19–20.
    2. Martin Norris, *Rolling Thunder: The Harley-Davidson Legend* (Philadelphia, PA: Courage Books, 1992), p. 15.
    3. Excerpt from a Harley-Davidson ad in *Motorcycle & Bicycle Illustrated,* April 13, 1922, from the collection of the Library of Congress. In the public domain.

Chapter 7

The Depression Years and Another War

It took about a year after the crash for the suffocating cloud of the Depression to settle across America. As thousands of banks failed, people lost their life savings. Factories closed left and right. A third of the railroad companies, the largest employer in the nation, went broke. Millions of people lost their jobs, and at the height of the Depression, over 30 percent of the population was unemployed. To make matters even worse, overseas markets for American goods began to dry up as well, as U.S. manufacturers had less and less to trade. Those that did faced high import tariffs as other countries scrambled to protect their own economies from the fallout. It was worse than awful.

The motorcycle industry was hit hard. Once cars became so affordable, motorcycles were considered more luxury items and were among the first to feel the pinch. In 1931, Excelsior threw in the towel and closed down for good. Harley and Indian were the only two motorcycle companies left standing. They continued the yearly pricing meetings they started in 1922 to keep prices at rock bottom, but by 1933, sales nationwide were only around 6,000—3,700 of them Harleys. Exports suffered, too. In 1929, about 40 percent of Harley's production went overseas. As the effects of the Depression spread beyond the United States, and heavy import taxes were slapped on motorcycles, exports dwindled to around 10 percent. Just as they did in the 1920s, the founders looked the challenge square in the eye and focused on new strategies to keep the company going.

STRATEGIC MOVE 1—DO SOMETHING CREATIVE TO BOLSTER OVERSEAS SALES

Enter Alfred Rich Child again. As you recall, he had set up a booming import business in Japan earlier in the 1920s. However, the Japanese economy was fluctuating and import taxes on U.S.-made Harleys kept going up. That gave Child another idea. Why not bypass imports altogether and build motorcycles right there in Japan? Under a $75,000 licensing agreement with the company back home, Child and the parent company of

Koto began to build the Shinagawa factory in 1929. Japan now had its very first motorcycle factory, complete with machines for parts production, tools, and blueprints for bikes, all provided by Harley-Davidson. In 1935, the first Japanese-made Harleys rolled out under the name Rikuo. Roughly translated, Rikuo means "King of the Road." Harley-Davidson ended the Japanese connection in 1937 because of licensing disagreements and the unstable Japanese government. By that time, Child had imported more than 23,000 motorcycles and overseen the production of thousands of Rikuos. Even though the company also cut its ties with the Shinagawa factory at the same time, it kept producing Rikuos until the late 1950s.

Joe Petrali—Harley's First Racing Superstar

Like most racing greats, Joe Petrali fell in love with motorcycles and motorcycle racing as a youngster. When he was old enough, he got a job in a motorcycle shop. There he learned the mechanical skills that would not only help him work on his own bikes over the years but that provided him with work after he left racing.

Joe Petrali—Harley's first racing superstar. Courtesy of Harley-Davidson Archives. Copyright Harley-Davidson.

He first began racing for Indian, and had several top finishes, but no victories. While with Indian, he became the first rider to race an alcohol-fueled motorcycle. He finished second in a pack of Harleys.

He got his break with Harley in 1925 when Ralph Hepburn was injured and told Petrali he could use his bike as long as he split the prize money with him. He won the board track race with an average speed of over 100 miles per hour, a record that stood unbroken. He kept his word and split the $1,000 winnings with Hepburn. Harley signed him to a formal contract and by the end of 1925, he was the national board track champion.

Petrali dominated the sport for the next 10 years. When Harley backed out of racing in 1926, he rode for Excelsior until it folded in 1931. He re-signed with Harley right away. That year he won eight dirt track and hill climb national championships, the only AMA rider in history to do that in the same year. In 1935, he won every single Class A race—ten in a row.

He enjoyed a big year in 1937. He broke the land speed record at Daytona on a streamlined Harley at a speed of over 136 miles per hour. A few months later, he won his 49th AMA national championship at a hill climb in Michigan.

He began cutting back on his racing in 1937, largely because Class A racing was giving way to Class C racing. Class A racing was truly professional racing with purpose-built motorcycles and skilled professional riders. Class C, however, was open to just about anybody with a motorcycle who wanted to race. He caved in one time in 1938 and entered a Class C race. The track was slick with oil, and riders were sliding and crashing into each other left and right. After he nearly got hit himself a few times, he pulled out of the race and walked away from racing forever. His record of 49 national championships stood until 1992 when Scott Parker passed him. Though his records have been broken, many consider the shy, soft-spoken Joe Petrali to be the greatest rider in the history of motorcycle racing.

STRATEGIC MOVE 2—KEEP EVERYBODY WORKING

The founders, especially William Davidson, had an almost sacred relationship with employees. Their unprecedented open-door management style was legendary. Many of the new manufacturing procedures and processes, as well as design innovations over the years, had grown from that relationship. Most employees had been with the company their whole working lives, and their skill and expertise were irreplaceable. The company didn't want to lose that.

The founders worked out a plan to avoid layoffs. In meetings with employees they came up with shorter work weeks and work-sharing plans.

Granted, it meant much smaller paychecks for everyone, but in those times, many other workers had no paycheck at all. The company dropped production of single cylinder motorcycles to focus solely on the v-twin. They limited production to commercial and overseas accounts, with a few motorcycles for general market. The plan worked well and everyone kept working.

STRATEGIC MOVE 3—FIGURE OUT WHAT'S NEEDED MOST RIGHT NOW

From the very beginning, the founders, especially Bill Harley and Arthur Davidson, had an uncanny knack for coming up with the next best thing for their customers. Call it an early example of "just in time" marketing. So, they took a close look at what might be needed most in austere times when everyone was looking for ways to get the most for whatever money they had. They ended up focusing their attention on commercial markets. The result of all this brainstorming was the 1932 Servi-Car.

In the early days, indeed up into the 1950s, car dealers made house calls to deliver new cars or make repairs. That generally meant taking two vehicles and a couple of drivers, which was a costly process during the Depression. But what if you were stuck out on some country road broken down or out of gas? Well, by then, phone lines had reached further out in the country, so you could always hike to the nearest house, pray that they had a phone, and, if they did, that the party line wasn't in use by the neighborhood's gossipmongers.

The Servi-Car was a three-wheeled 750 cc v-twin 45 with two wide-set wheels in the rear that could carry a fairly large container. It was fitted with a tow bar and heavy-duty battery. The mechanic's tools and an extra can of gasoline fit easily into the big trunk on back. The extra wide stance of the rear wheels matched the track of automobiles and made navigating rutted roads easier. They were easier to handle and more stable than a two-wheeler, so they were perfect for new or inexperienced riders. They were tough and reliable and made the most of a gallon of gas in times when every penny counted. They were less expensive to operate and easier to maintain than a car and got the job done just as well.

Arthur's marketing team pitched the Servi-Car to car dealers everywhere as a cost-efficient, reliable way to get the same job done without all the extra cars. One driver could deliver the car, towing the Servi-Car behind, then ride the Servi-Car back to the shop. Same for repairs—one vehicle, one driver, and a trunk full of tools would slash overhead for the dealers.

They were a hit from the start. Car dealers started ordering them right away. It wasn't long before independent garages caught on and began buying Servi-Cars as well. Police forces and delivery-based businesses put in their orders, too. For a few extra bucks, a buyer could add the police department or business logo, hand-painted at the factory before delivery.

1932 Servi-Car. From the author's private collection.

The Servi-Car required no special adjustments in production processes. It used the same engine and components used in other bikes, so it
could ride down the same assembly line. That meant the company could
offer the dealers a higher profit margin, which, of course, made the dealers
very happy. Happy dealers made enthusiastic salespeople. The Servi-Car
was a smashing success and stayed in production until 1974.

STRATEGIC MOVE 4—SPRUCE UP THE EXISTING LINE

Motorcycles were already considered luxury items, so instead of adding a new model, the company turned to the "look" of the bikes. In 1931,
chrome became an option. In 1932, the standard dull army green and variations thereof gave way to vibrant new colors like peach and aqua or yel-
low along with two-tones and pin striping as custom options. By 1933, all
the gas tanks sported a stylized art-deco eagle.

Color and chrome options were available long before the Depression,
but only if a customer asked. They weren't advertised or offered in the
company catalogue. In the early 1930s, however, they went public—in
ads, the catalogues, and in articles in *The Enthusiast*. It was the official beginning of Harley's factory custom division, an industry first.

In a way, these new custom options added to the notion of individuality and self-expression that ads in the 1920s had started to cultivate. Be
your own person. Paint your bike any color you want. Be free. Be different.

Harley Team Racing in the 1930s and 1940s

1930   Bill Davidson Jr. (young Bill) won the 420-mile Jack Pine En-
         duro run with a near perfect score.

1932   Joe Petrali launched a five-year winning streak of AMA Grand
         National Championships and a four-year streak of National
         Hill-Climb Championships.

Happy Seamans at a hillclimb in New York in 1936. Courtesy of Harley-Davidson Archives.
Copyright Harley-Davidson.

1933 Joe Petrali won all thirteen AMA National Championship dirt track races and broke four records on a Harley Peashooter.

1937 Joe Petrali set a new land speed record of over 136 miles per hour on a Harley WL 61 overhead valve Knuckle-head. He broke the record for 45 cubic inch engines the same day.

1938 Ben Campanale won the first of two in a row at the Daytona.

1940 Babe Trancrede won the Daytona 200.

1947 Jimmy Chann won the first of three in a row AMA Grand National dirt track Championships.

Be wild. Another subtle build on the Harley mystique that is such a huge part of the brand image today.

Harley Women: 1930s and 1940s

Arthur's ad campaigns aimed at women in the 1920s meant more women were riding motorcycles in the 1930s and 1940s. Motorcycle clubs just for women started to sprout up, led by the Motor Maids, organized in the late 1930s by Wellesley grad Linda Dugeau, and officially chartered in 1941. It was the first official women's motorcycle club in the world.

STRATEGIC MOVE 5—GET THE DEALERS MORE INVOLVED AND BUILD A SPIRIT OF CAMARADERIE

Part of Arthur's rigorous training of new dealers and salespeople had always revolved around making customers feel at home whether they were there to buy a motorcycle or not. Training included follow up with existing customers to see how things were going and pick up new ideas they could pass on to the company. During the Depression, dealers began to more vigorously promote visits to their shops as times to chat and make new friends, have a cup of tea, look at the bikes, maybe even take a test drive even if nobody had a penny in their pockets. It was a spirit-lifting gesture in times when spirits were low. And it built up a boatload of good will for Harley-Davidson.

The company had openly encouraged clubs and rallies for years. It urged dealers to sponsor special events under the Harley banner. It stepped up these efforts during the Depression. It certainly helped to build on the strong bond already growing among Harley owners and enthusiasts and brought new customers into the fold. Motorcycle riding clubs had been around since the beginning, and the company openly encouraged them, especially during the Depression. Load a buddy in a sidecar, fire up your machine, and take off with like-minded friends to get away from it all, even if you only had enough gas money to make it two miles out of town and back. They knew that encouraging the spirit of friendship among riders and future riders would translate into sales when the rough times were over. It also added yet another subtle layer to the fledgling Harley mystique. Adventure, freedom, and the fellowship of kindred spirits. It was balm for the soul in very trying times.

The First Harley Motorcycle Club

The Yonkers Motorcycle Club grew out of the Yonkers Bicycle Club, founded in the late 1800s by George Eller. Club members were soon riding Harleys instead of bicycles. The club sponsored endurance runs and served as civil defense couriers during World War II. The club is alive and well today, still sponsoring charity races, and still riding Harleys.

Just like the strategies of the 1920s, the company's strategies this time around paid off. Slowly, but surely, sales began to rise. By 1934 sales were up around 10,000 and climbing. The rest of the country was also beginning to recover, largely because of the New Deal.

The New Deal grew out of a 1932 campaign promise from Franklin D. Roosevelt, Democratic governor of New York, when he accepted his party's nomination to run for President of the United States. He told a Depression-weary America that "I pledge you, I pledge myself, to a new deal for the American people."[1] After his landslide election, his administration pushed through new banking laws, the Social Security Act, and a number of programs for direct relief and to put people back to work through such programs as the Works Progress Administration (WPA) and the Civil Conservation Corps (CCC). The CCC alone put millions to work planting trees and building nearly 100,000 miles of roads.

By 1939, the country was pulling out of the depression and the New Deal programs began to go by the wayside as more and more people went back to work at other jobs, but it had served its purpose. It was the first instance of the federal government stepping in on a comprehensive scale to meet a widespread challenge that touched nearly every aspect of American life. It also set the stage for future government social and economic welfare programs.[2]

As people began to have a little money to spend, manufacturing slowly rumbled back to life. People began to buy motorcycles again, many of them folks who had been among those visitors to the dealerships during the hard times. A new optimism began to spread around the country and eventually made its way around the world. Overseas markets began to order American goods again, including motorcycles.

WE MIGHT BEND, BUT WE DON'T BREAK

It's pretty obvious by now that Harley-Davidson was a unique company and not just because of the motorcycles it produced. It was financially sound, even when sales plummeted, because of Walter's frugal management of company funds. Its employees were loyal as well as skilled because they were valued as part of the team—a principle that William nurtured from day one. Arthur's marketing team was insightful as well as clever, even when there seemed to be no market at all. And Bill Harley's head was full of creative ideas just waiting to rumble off the assembly line when the time was right. All these divergent skills came together for a common goal. The founders weren't afraid to take chances or make bold moves into uncharted territory, but they weren't reckless about it. From top to bottom it was a disciplined, well-coordinated team that combined vision, practicality, and courage in the face of challenges that destroyed most of its competition.

INTRODUCTION OF AN AMERICAN CLASSIC

Heralding a new era in Harley-Davidson history, the 61E model debuted in 1936. This 1000 cc v-twin had the first recirculating oil system, which was a very big deal. Prior to this, riders had to hand lubricate the engine by means of a squeeze pump. Even though the new oiling system tended to be a little leaky, it was still a huge improvement and heartily welcomed by riders old and new. The 61E also featured a 4-speed gear box, and could do 90 miles per hour, no sweat. It had overhead valves that gave it the extra power without sacrificing efficiency. It was the first overhead valve motorcycle engine made in the United States and would set the standard for Harley production for years to come. It soon became known as the Knucklehead because of the knobby engine covers. In 1937, factory racing legend Joe Petrali set a new land speed record of over 136 miles per hour on a modified Knucklehead. To this day, old timers speak of the Knucklehead with misty-eyed reverence.

Two new side-valve v-twins came out about the same time with 1200 cc and 1400 cc engines. They were tough and powerful and easy to maintain. The chunky 30 horsepower engines were just right for sidecars and police work. They were the perfect complement to the sportier Knucklehead. The company also kept producing the side-valve 750 cc D 45 to power the Servi-Cars that were becoming more and more popular. This model eventually morphed into the WL, and finally into the WLA used by the army in World War II.

THE BEGINNING OF TWO LEGENDARY MEET-UPS—
DAYTONA BIKE WEEK AND THE STURGIS RALLY

January 1937 saw the first running of the Daytona 200 motorcycle race in Daytona Beach, Florida. The race course was a combination of roads and hard sand on the beach. An Indian motorcycle, averaging a little over 70 miles per hour, won the race. Racing was suspended between 1942 and 1947 because of the war, but people still came to party for the week. Today, Bike Week is a 10-day event, usually held in late February and early March.

Harley-Davidson has played a role in Bike Week since the beginning. At least one of the founders made the ride down from Milwaukee every year. The factory racing team enjoyed many victories over the years, boosting Harley's image with the performance crowd.

In 1938 the Jackpine Gypsies Motorcycle Club in Sturgis, South Dakota, organized motorcycle races called the Black Hills Motor Classic. It was such a success that it has continued every year since, except for 1942 when gas was rationed during the war. It eventually became known as the Sturgis Rally and today attracts 500,000 people for the week-long event in July and August.

As with Daytona, Harley-Davidson has been and continues to be a prominent player. Both events have always been excellent times for networking and mingling with riders and customers to get feedback and pick up on ideas.

Harley-Davidson and the Police: A Long and Fruitful Partnership

When the first Harley Silent Grey Fellow reported for police duty in Detroit in 1908, it began a long history of police sales that eventually extended around the world. From the very beginning, the advantages of using motorcycles were obvious—they were faster and easier to get around on, could maneuver through town traffic better than horses, and they were economical to operate. Harley's reputation for toughness and reliability made the choice a no-brainer.

During the 1920s, police sales surged while civilian sales fell drastically. These were the times of prohibition, and many a moonshiner found a motorcycle cop on his tail as he made his midnight deliveries over the rough rural roads. With more cars on the roads, and nobody paying any attention to speed limits, quick and maneuverable motorcycles were just the thing for chasing down speeders. In 1921 in Washington State, the first state troopers were sworn in, all of them on Harleys. More states followed suit, and in 1926, the company created a special department just for police sales.

The stock market crash and subsequent Great Depression hit Harley as hard as everyone else, and sales fell. However, sales to police departments helped keep them afloat. The Servi-Car, which came out

Early 1930s policeman on his 1200 cc VL. From the collection of OnlyClassics.

in 1932, added another dimension to police sales and remained in the police fleet line-up until 1971.

In the 1940s, Harley teamed up with Northwestern University's Center for Public Safety to provide officer training. That strong relationship continues today. Harley also began publishing the *Mounted Officer*, a magazine dedicated to motorcycle police everywhere.

Teens in the 1950s and 1960s got to know cops riding Harleys very well. Street racing and street drags were the big thing, and police departments began to dedicate motorcycle squads to deal with them.

Today, Harley is still the bike of choice for more than 3,400 police departments in the United States and 45 countries worldwide.

UNIONS COME KNOCKING ON HARLEY'S DOOR

Unions had been around for a long time before the Depression, but they weren't very well organized, didn't carry much clout, and membership was scanty. As unemployment began to rise in the 1920s and crested in the enormous wave of the early 1930s, unions got their acts together and started to become a force in the workplace. By the mid-1930s, many industrial shops had joined unions, and it wasn't long before union talk was circulating on the Harley assembly line. Given the unique relationship between employees and management at Harley, you'd think unionizing would be the last thing on their minds. They were paid well, the company had kept them working during the dark years, and there was mutual respect unmatched in the manufacturing world. Many of them wanted nothing to do with the union, but enough of them did to create a majority in favor of unionizing.

Needless to say, the founders were stunned and fought the effort tooth and nail. It was also a hard emotional hit for William, who had worked side-by-side with these same people for so long. He probably felt that, in some ways, it was a betrayal of trust and loyalty. But there was no stopping it. In 1937, William signed the agreement, and Harley-Davidson became a union shop. William died of a heart attack two days later. Some say it was the stress of the whole business that did him in. But I think he simply died of a broken heart.

The Second Generation Steps Up

By the 1930s, several of the founders' sons had joined the company, starting on the shop floor. Other family members and relatives had become stockholders. William's son, also named William but known as "young Bill," was already winning endurance races for the company. William's death in 1937 marked the beginning of the end of an era, but the dynasty would continue, at least in part.

THE WORLD AT WAR AGAIN

In 1939, war with Germany broke out again, and moved like wildfire across Europe and Great Britain. Unlike the previous war, this one was truly global, as Australia, New Zealand, Canada, and others all declared war against Germany. As German U-boats patrolled the Atlantic, including the coasts of the United States, no international shipping lanes were safe. Russia declared war on Germany, and Japan joined the German axis. Americans started getting edgy. Relations with Japan were shaky already, and after the Pearl Harbor bombing in 1941, the United States declared war on Japan and officially joined the fray.

Training Wartime Bikers

During the war, each motorcycle was generally assigned to one person. Sometimes it was hard to find GIs to ride motorcycles because so few had driver's licenses. Bill Harley's son, Lt. John Harley, was stationed at the Armed Forces School and given the job of finding qualified riders and training them for wartime riding. He toured the country (on a Harley, of course), networking with American Motorcyclist Association clubs to find members who were also in the military. Resourceful lad. Like his daddy.

Harley-Davidson was involved in the war effort long before Pearl Harbor. German bombs had wiped out all the British motorcycle factories, and both Harley and Indian shipped out several thousand motorcycles for the British army. Harley's entry was the 750 cc 45 WL with a few modifications designed to stand up to its tough wartime assignment. Russia soon ordered bikes, and Australia got several thousand under the Lend-Lease program.

Once the United States entered the war, orders for army motorcycles started pouring in and factory production shifted almost exclusively to the wartime effort. The company service school once again became the Quartermaster school to train army mechanics. The bike of choice was the 750 cc 45 WL, dubbed the WLA (A for army). It was standard drab army green, with bigger, knobby tires, more protection for the oil pump, and big mud guards. The company tuned the engine down a bit, which made it a little slower but gave it more pulling power for the varied terrain it would be facing.

Score Another One for Bill Harley

The army had originally approached Harley about building 500 cc motorcycles for the war. That would have required a pretty big shift in machining at the factory, an investment in time and money the founders didn't want at all. Savvy negotiator that he was, Bill Harley convinced the army that a 500 cc bike would be too wimpy for the rough conditions on the front. They needed something tougher. Besides, the company already had the 750 cc bike in production, so even with the few modifications that would be needed, they could get them out almost immediately because there would be no delay for retooling and resetting production schedules. The army bought it, higher price and all. The WLA became the motorcycle of World War II. To top it all off, the company was given four Army-Navy "E" awards for their wartime production efforts.

In late 1942, when the allies were chasing German General Rommel, the Desert Fox, all across North Africa, the army put in a special order for a custom-made motorcycle. It was actually a little insulting, to tell the truth. They asked the company to base the design on the German BMW flat twin that Rommel was using so successfully to evade allied forces. Even though the company was reluctant at first, the army had plenty of money to spend thanks to a big jump in defense funding. The company was more than happy to help them spend it and came up with the 750 cc XA. They delivered about a thousand of them before the North African offensive ended, and that was the end of the XA. Legend has it, though, that there are still XAs buried in the shifting sands of North Africa.

By the time the war ended in 1945, Harley had shipped out 90,000 motorcycles, 30,000 of them to Russia and 20,000 to Canada, and thousands more to other allies under the Lend-Lease program. They made money. Sales of motorcycles, sidecars, and parts for the war effort put Harley at the top of the worldwide motorcycle heap once again.

Almost as important as the money was the high visibility of Harleys during the war. They were everywhere, and the name and reputation got a better boost than any advertising could buy. European civilians wanted them and there would have been a tremendous market there. Unfortunately, European governments had levied hefty import taxes on foreign goods as they struggled to rebuild their own shattered industries. That jacked the price of a new Harley up out of the reach of most new riders.

It took a while for the company to get back into full civilian production. Raw materials were hard to come by at first, domestic manufacturers were plagued by a rash of union strikes, and the cost of exporting was hardly worth the trouble. Although Harley continued to export motorcycles, the numbers dropped drastically. The company did, however, put out a 750 cc model in 1946 strictly for the race track, but not for the general public. By 1947 materials shortages eased, production cranked up again, and in 1948, the company sold over 31,000 motorcycles, some of them undelivered surplus from the war. A huge chunk of their new customer base was returning servicemen who wanted the bikes they'd ridden in war. Good thing, too. They also had a huge surplus of parts and components and could whip together a WLA in a heartbeat.

The Hummer: The Spoils of War

As part of the reparations following World War II, Germany was forced to give up designs for most of its major manufacturing processes, including the plans for the DKW. All of the allies got copies. Harley used its set to create the Hummer. British maker BSA used theirs to create the Bantam, which would later challenge Harley's market in America.

Things were going well enough that the company felt comfortable with expanding its facilities. In 1947 it bought an old propeller plant that sprang up for the war effort then closed when the war ended. The company converted it to a machine shop to produce engines and transmissions for the main assembly building.

Another Classic

In 1947, the Harley accessories catalogue introduced the black leather jacket.

In 1947, dealers started asking for lighter weight bikes that would be good for young riders or riders who wanted something to get around on that wasn't so heavy and got better gas mileage. Harley responded in 1948 with a 125 cc single-cylinder two-stroke model based on the German DKW. It weighed only 175 pounds compared to the 600-pound Knucklehead, and it got 90 miles to the gallon. They called it the Hummer and sold 10,000 of them in 1948.

In 1948 the 1000 cc and 1200 cc overhead valve models got some upgrades, and the knobby Knucklehead engine covers were replaced with covers that looked like upside-down pie pans. No surprise that the new look earned the nickname Panhead. This was the beginning of what would become known as the Evolution engine in the future. In 1949, the Panhead got a makeover including hydraulic telescoping front forks to replace the Springer forks and became known as the Hydra-Glide.

A New Tradition

Through the years, customers had given the bikes their names like the Knucklehead, Panhead, and Hummer. Except for the Silent Grey Fellow, the company just designated models by numbers and letters, if that much. The company broke with tradition in 1949 by naming the Hydra-Glide right from the start.

THE TORCH PASSES

Neither Bill Harley nor Walter Davidson lived to see the end of the war. Walter died in 1942, Bill in 1943. It was a devastating loss for the company. William's son, young Bill, became president of the company. He had started working there in 1928 after graduating with honors from the University of Wisconsin with a degree in business. He started on the shop floor, worked his way up to foreman, then to manager of several different departments. He knew the company well. He also knew motorcycles. He'd been riding since he was a youngster, began racing as a teenager, and won the Jack Pine Enduro in 1930. He rode his bike to work every day. With Arthur as his mentor, it was young Bill who led the company through World War II, through the postwar lull, and into the up and down times that lay ahead.

WHISPERS OF THINGS TO COME

Even though foreign markets imposed high taxes on imports, U.S. taxes on imports were quite low. As a result, the United States was soon flooded with foreign goods produced by cheap labor with lower prices than American-made goods. That included motorcycles. One-third of the new motorcycles sold in the United States in 1946 were British models. For the first time, Harley faced foreign competition on its home turf. It didn't look good. Not good at all.

Timeline for the Depression and War Years

1931   Excelsior called it quits and closed down for good. Harley-Davidson's only competition was Indian.

        The company offered chrome as a factory option.

1932   The 750 cc, three-wheel Servi-Car rolled out and was a hit with car dealers, garages, police forces, and delivery businesses.

        The company offered paint color and detailing options on all models. It marked the official beginning of Harley-Davidson factory custom work.

1933   The U.S. economy had tanked out fully and Harley sold only 3,700 motorcycles that year.

        To keep its people working, the company reduced hours, implemented work-sharing programs, dropped single-cylinder models, and produced motorcycles almost exclusively for overseas or commercial markets.

        The art-deco eagle became standard on all gas tanks.

1934   Sales began to recover and went over 10,000 by the end of the year.

1935   Under a $75,000 dollar licensing agreement, Japan produced its first motorcycles—Harleys with the name Rikuo.

1936   Harley introduced the 1000 cc Knucklehead. Also new were the 1000 cc and 1200 cc side valve workhorses that became a big hit with police departments.

1937   The Harley-Davidson shop became a union shop over fierce objections from the founders.

        William Davidson died two days after signing the union agreement.

1939   War broke out again in Europe, and Harley began supplying allies with motorcycles.

1941   The United States joined the war effort after Pearl Harbor, and Harley shifted production almost exclusively to military contracts. By the end of the war, Harley supplied the U.S. military and the Allies with 90,000 motorcycles.

        The company service school began training army mechanics.

1942   Harley produced the XA 750 for desert use in North Africa. Only 1,000 were produced and the contract was canceled when that part of the war ended.

Walter Davidson died. William's son, young Bill, became president of the company.

1943   Bill Harley died. Arthur Davidson was the last of the founders still standing.

1946   One-third of the bikes sold in the United States were imported from the UK. Bad omen.

1947   The company bought another building for a machine shop to produce parts.

The black leather jacket appeared for the first time anywhere in the Harley accessories catalogue.

1948   The Knucklehead got a makeover and became the Panhead, the beginning of what would become the Evolution engines of the future.

The company debuted a new lightweight 125 cc two-stroke single-cylinder bike called the Hummer that got 90 miles to the gallon.

1949   The Panhead got hydraulic telescoping front forks and became known as the Hydra-Glide.

NOTES

1. Library of Congress, "Great Depression and World War II, 1929–1945: President Franklin Delano Roosevelt and the New Deal, 1933–1945," *American Memory*, 2004, http://memory.loc.gov/learn/features/timeline/depwwii/newdeal/newdeal.html (last accessed August 22, 2007). In the public domain.
2. Ibid.

Chapter 8

Years of Challenge and Change: The 1950s

Americans greeted the 1950s feeling pretty darn good. The economy was strong, factories were humming, more people than ever were working, and they had extra money to spend. Young couples were buying houses and cars and making babies. The Baby Boom generation was in full swing.

Life in general was very different from just 15 years before. The New Deal projects in the 1930s created a nationwide network of paved roads, and all but the most remote country roads were at least gravel. The Rural Electrification Program in the 1930s and 1940s meant just about everybody had "lights." Electric refrigerators replaced the drippy, messy ice boxes, and most people cooked with gas or electricity instead of wood. Washing machines, vacuum cleaners, central heat, and indoor plumbing crept in over the years. People went to the movies, and there was a new thing called television. Life was much sweeter. Long gone were those harsh, early days when Bill and Arthur cobbled together their first motorcycle in the Davidson basement.

Life was good in Milwaukee, too. Motorcycle sales had been climbing since the war. Cars weren't threats any longer. Just about everybody had one, and the people who wanted motorcycles bought them whether they had a car or not. If anything, Harley-Davidson could look back at the challenges presented by the automobile as inspiration for some of their most creative design and advertising work. The Servi-Car was just one example. It was the perfect combination of anticipating customer need (a cost-efficient, reliable way to get a job done), using a proven commodity as the base (the D 45 motorcycle), and using clever marketing that set the competition (the car) up as the foil to point out all the advantages of the new product. During the 1930s and 1940s, Harley-Davidson had pretty much retired the trophies for flawless teamwork and ingenuity in the face of impending disaster.

Because most people had cars, motorcycles were no longer primary modes of transportation and had become more luxury items than necessities. That shift had driven most bike makers into oblivion, but not Harley. Thanks to Arthur's brilliant marketing campaign over the years, the Harley-Davidson brand had come to mean more than utility and economy.

It had taken on the aura of lifestyle and personal expression. People bought Harleys for what they stood for as much as for what they could do.

The 1950s dawned on a high note of optimism at Harley-Davidson. Sales were good, dealers were sponsoring successful events that brought in new customers, and the factory race team was bringing home one national championship after another. The year ended on a note of grief when Arthur and his wife were killed in a car wreck on December 30. The last of the original bright lights snuffed out, Harley-Davidson became a second-generation company.

A couple of other dark clouds were hovering on the horizon, too. They began forming in the late 1940s, but didn't get much serious attention then. But they didn't go away, and by the early 1950s were starting to be problems. Big problems that got bigger in the coming years.

PROBLEM 1: BAD BOYS

Nobody thought much about it when a few young rowdies here and there started taking the mufflers off their bikes and thundering through neighborhoods in packs. Nor was there much more than a fleeting cuss word at daredevil bikers weaving in and out of traffic causing drivers to slam on the brakes and lay on the horn. They were annoying, and putting themselves at risk, but beyond that, nothing to get worried about. The problem for Milwaukee was that most of them were riding Harleys. But even the company didn't pay much attention to it either. You know, boys will be boys.

The July 4, 1947, American Motorcyclist Association (AMA) clubman's rally in Hollister, California, spawned an event that was much more ominous. Over 4,000 motorcyclists turned out for the 2-day rally, among them a few hundred malcontents on stripped down Harleys loaded up with beer. The group decided to take on the town, and the ensuing mayhem attracted national press attention. Whether it really was a riot as portrayed in the press or not, it did take several hundred policemen to get things under control. The press had a field day. And wouldn't you know it, a photo of a drunken biker slouched on his Harley, waving a beer bottle at the camera made the cover of *Life* magazine.

The AMA, a close ally of Harley-Davidson, quickly denounced the incident as an unfortunate but isolated event. They just as quickly pointed out that 99 percent of riders were respectable, law-abiding citizens and this one percent of ne'er-do-wells was a disgusting aberration. Harley-riding movie stars added their voices, condemning the bad behavior, and posed for positive publicity photos on their Harleys. Sociologists and psychologists chalked it up as a legacy of the war that left many young men disillusioned, emotionally shattered, and unable to meet society's norms. Whatever the commentary, one thing was clear. A new breed of biker had been born. And they were riding Harleys.

Harley Team Racing in the 1950s

1950   Larry Headrick won the AMA Grand National Dirt Track Championship.

Harley won 18 National Championships and set a batch of new racing records.

1954   Harley started an eight-year Grand National Dirt Track Championship streak.

1955   Another winning streak began. This time was a seven-year string of first place wins at Daytona. All victories came on KR model racing bikes.

1958   Carroll Resweber won the first of his four AMA Grand National Championships.

The AMA did their best to counter the bad publicity. Ads for rallies featured clean-cut groups of riders with smiling families and announced prizes for well turned-out clubs, most outstanding motorcycle, and other upscale, harmless activities. Harley continued to focus its advertising on the respectability of motorcycling with ads featuring well-dressed riders enjoying the beauty of the great outdoors. Ads captured images of fresh-faced young people in swimsuits at the beach posing with their Harleys, or jolly groups gathered around a campfire with Harleys parked nearby. They continued to play up the incredible winning ways of the Wrecking Crew at the racetrack. All of it probably helped take the sting out of Hollister for a little while.

The One Percenters

Some clubs wanted nothing to do with the clean-cut image and proudly anointed themselves as one percenters. Some clubs even began adding a diamond shaped patch with "1%" embroidered on it to add to the club patches on their vests. They considered it a badge of honor. They argued that being a one percenter just meant that they were committed to biking and brotherhood as a way of life and not just the occasional weekend thing. They felt that law enforcement agencies had unfairly singled them out as criminals just because they were different. Today, law enforcement groups consider four one-percenter clubs as true outlaw gangs: the Hells Angels, the Pagans, the Outlaws, and the Bandidos. Even among the ranks of these clubs, members will argue that very few of them are law-breakers and they're being singled out unfairly. Rowdy sometimes? Yes. Nonconformists? For sure. But criminals? No way.

The Hollister fiasco inspired the 1954 classic movie, *The Wild One,* starring young Marlon Brando and Lee Marvin. It was loosely based on Hollister, but was more a movie about a young man's quest for love and the meaning of life. It was still a movie about bad boy bikers, even though Marlon Brando's character was a loveable bad boy. Unfortunately, he rode a Triumph. Lee Marvin's character was the classic nasty bad boy. He rode a Harley.

The movie was a smash and spawned a rash of outlaw biker movies in the next few years. Most of them were truly dreadful but played to packed houses. Rebellious youngsters latched on to black leather jackets, Harley caps, and motorcycle boots and swaggered their way through their youth whether they had a motorcycle or not. And you can bet a lot of them got their gear through the Harley accessories catalogue. Remember? Harley first introduced the black leather jacket as fashionable riding garb back in the 1940s. The black leather cap, too.

Like it or not, the outlaw biker became a symbol for young rebels. Although the Harley brand got a little smudge, it wasn't tarnished. There was no significant impact on sales, so nobody in Milwaukee lost much sleep over it. Besides, in the 1950s, there were bigger fish to fry—growing competition from foreign brands in the American market that *was* cutting into Harley sales.

Harley Women—The 1950s

Dot Robinson was just a 5'2" wisp of a girl and started riding Harleys in the 1930s as a teenager. By the late 1930s, she was riding endurance races. In 1937, she finished second in the bone-breaking two-day Jack Pine Enduro Run. She came back the next year to win it. That was a *very* big deal.

She was the first president of the Motor Maids and, during the 1940s and 1950s, rode thousands of miles every year to promote the club. Her appearances at AMA events and dealer rallies, as well as her much-publicized travels on her Harley, went a long way to boost the image of respectable riding in the 1950s. She said that by the end of her riding days, she had covered about 1.5 million miles!

PROBLEM 2: THE FOREIGN MOTORCYCLE INVASION

Since 1946 there had been an ever-increasing stream of British-made motorcycles flowing into the United States. In the early 1950s, U.S. manufacturers still faced high import taxes in foreign ports, but foreign importers enjoyed outrageously low taxes on goods shipped to the United States. To add insult to injury, makes like BSA, Triumph, and Norton were lighter with smaller engine capacity (500 cc), yet their single and twin engines matched the performance of both Harley and Indian. They had hand clutches and foot pedal gear shifts. They were fast, looked sharp, and were cheaper. By 1950, they were selling like crazy and making a dent in Harley's market.

Dealers had been asking Milwaukee when they could expect a bike to meet the British middleweight challenge since the late 1940s. The company had the 125 cc and 165 cc Hummers that sold well to beginning riders, but it was sadly lacking anything in between the Hummers and the big "hogs." Its customers wanted something sportier, faster, and lighter, and it was losing business. To make matters worse, the company refused to allow its dealers to service imports, sell parts—even tires—to owners of imports, or stock the very popular little American-made Cushman motor scooter to help boost sales. It was Harley or nothing. Several dealers abandoned ship and opened dealerships for the competition.

Where Was Indian All This Time?

Indian was feeling the pinch of the British invasion as well. Unlike Harley, however, it was not financially stable enough to try and tough it out. Almost immediately, it began to switch its production to smaller bikes that could compete in the middleweight market. Only a few bikes came out before production costs went up. Indian couldn't find backers to finance them and had lost dealers to Harley or the British makers. A few poor management decisions and a near-empty bank account forced the company to close down for good in 1953, leaving Harley-Davidson as the only U.S. motorcycle maker.

The company seemed unwilling or unable to immediately focus on producing a motorcycle to challenge the British. Advertisements continued to play up Harley's reputation for reliability and durability, the joys of open road travel on the comfortable Hydra-Glide, and the kinship of Harley riders as a group. Executives kept up the pressure on dealers to sponsor events and gatherings to bring riders together and welcome new customers. It was a formula that worked well in the past, but these were different times with different challenges. They needed to come up with a motorcycle that could compete.

Instead, they turned to Washington for help. They petitioned the U.S. Tariff Commission to impose a 40 percent import tax on foreign-made motorcycles and to restrict shipments to prewar levels. Importers banded together for the 1951 Senate hearings, among them Alfred Rich Child. Child had split from Harley-Davidson after the company cut ties in Japan, and had picked up U.S. distribution rights for BSA in 1945. At the hearing he spoke eloquently of Harley's failure to produce a middleweight machine to match the competition, its heavy-handed tactics with dealers, and he accused the company of trying to control the market and drive out competition. Harley got no help from the feds. Request denied.

FINALLY, A CHALLENGER . . . SORT OF

In 1952, Harley rolled out the K model. It had many of the new mechanical features of the British bikes, and a sleeker, sportier look. In fact, some of the styling features were almost identical. Problem was, it was still a 750 cc machine, and it was slower than its competitors. It sold OK, but not great. The next step was the KH, with an even bigger engine (883 cc) and more power. The last of the K group was the KHK, whose engine modifications made this one the fastest of the lot, with a top speed of 95 miles per hour. With some tweaking here and there, the newer, faster versions got a better reception, but none of them was blowing anybody away. Drag racing was hot, so the younger generation of riders was looking for higher performance, a quick start off the line at a stop light, and a bike that was lighter on its feet than the bigger Harleys. They kept on buying BSA, Triumph, and Norton.

The KR racing version appeared in 1953. Even though Harley was taking a hit in the public markets, it was still successful at the races, but the British were gaining ground. The KR changed all that. From its first burst out of the gate, the KR was a winner and kept the Wrecking Crew on top for a number of years to come.

Although sales overall were down, the little Hummers and heavyweights like the Hydra-Glide sold well, and police and commercial accounts were strong, keeping Harley financially sound. Apparently, it felt it could take its own sweet time coming up with just the right bike. In a big display of confidence, Harley threw a 50th anniversary bash in 1953 complete with a commemorative medallion attached to the front fender of every new bike produced that year.

ANOTHER SMACK DOWN FROM THE FEDS

Harley dealers were getting restless and unhappy, to put it politely. They still had nothing to sell their customers asking for middleweight bikes and were losing sales. They were still expected to sponsor events and get-togethers at their own expense when their funds were dwindling. Because of the company's demands of exclusivity, they couldn't even offer parts and service on other makes to fill in the gap. Maybe the complaints came from dealers. Maybe they came from the competition. Whatever the source, the complaints landed in Washington, and once again, the company found itself in the hot seat. In 1954 the Federal Trade Commission (FTC) ruled that Harley Davidson was trying to create a monopoly and discourage competition—practices that violated antitrust laws. The FTC ordered the company to end its exclusivity demands on dealers immediately. The ruling left the door wide open for Harley dealers to carry competitive brands, service all brands of motorcycles, and add parts and accessories other than Harley. And that's exactly what they did. Harleys began to stand shoulder-to-shoulder in dealer showrooms with BSAs, Triumphs, and Nortons. It was a crushing blow.

1957—IT'S A KEEPER!

Eleven years after the first British bikes started trickling into the United States, Harley came up with an honest-to-goodness challenger. They took an overhead-valve top, slipped it on to the 883 cc K engine, snuggled it all into the K frame, added a distinctive peanut tank, and called it the XL Sportster. It was lean, mean, and sounded like a beast. It was an instant hit and became the first of the Harley superbikes. The 1958 version was even better, with a top speed of 125 miles per hour and a quarter mile time of 14 seconds. The musclebike boys had a performance powerhouse that was quick off the line, fast on the long stretch, and built Harley tough. The Sportster was a looker too, with all the styling of the British bikes done up Harley style. The Sportster endures to this day as one of Harley's most popular motorcycles.

Elvis Presley: The Original Outlaw

In 1955, young Elvis was just starting to make some real money in the music business. He bought his first Harley—a 165 cc ST (the larger version of the Hummer). It didn't take him long to become an accomplished rider, and less than a year later, he traded in his 165 for a 1956 KH, complete with windshield and buddy seat. In May 1956, he was the "cover boy" for Harley's *Enthusiast* magazine, riding his KH and tipping his white-brimmed black leather Harley cap to the camera. By the end of the year, he had bought an even bigger bike—a 1957 Hydra-Glide. Elvis bought dozens of Harleys during his lifetime. Once he was making mega-zillions, every time he bought a new bike for himself, he bought one for each of his entourage as well. Elvis didn't like to ride alone.

So what made Elvis the original outlaw? Remember my definition of outlaw in the Preface? Well, Elvis was that and more. He was a clean-cut, well-dressed, good-looking guy with a great career. He was polite and soft-spoken. He loved his family, never ran afoul of the law, and for just about every rock album he put out, he also put out a gospel album. Just look at how he's dressed in the picture here. That's how he dressed most of the time when he went out riding, with the addition of his leather jacket and Harley cap. Squeaky clean.

The freedom-loving wild child in Elvis was the one who got on stage, made his own style of music, swiveled his hips, gyrated like a crazy man, and drove women nuts. The wild child also loved motorcycles, and he gave it free rein every time he got on his Harley. He loved the wind in his face, and the thrill of thundering down the road on a big hog. And like a true Harley rider, he loved to have his friends

Elvis Presley on a police model Duo-Glide. From the author's private collection.

along with him, whether riding behind on the buddy seat or as part of the pack on their own Harleys. Yep. Elvis was class and individuality—an outlaw in the truest sense of the word.

By the way, the Harley-Davidson Motor Company now owns Elvis's original KH, to be displayed proudly in their new museum opening in 2008.

In 1958 the Panhead Hydra-Glide became the Duo-Glide, with hydraulic suspension added to the rear end for a smoother ride, more comfortable seats, rear brakes and choice of hand or lever gear shift. They were the first big cruising bikes with both front and rear hydraulic suspension and rear brakes. They were a hit with the long distance road trippers and an even bigger hit with police departments.

NOTICED SOMETHING MISSING?

As we've traveled through the challenges of the 1950s, have you noticed something different about the way the company handled them? Remember back to the ways the founders handled falling sales in the 1920s, the threat of the automobile, and the Depression years. Each time, they came up with a plan. They sought input from everyone—workers, dealers, and customers. They devised a set of strategies and everyone in the company helped set those strategies in motion. It was a unified effort fueled by the strength of a unified vision. We didn't see that this time, did we? How come? Let's just toss around a few ideas.

The Original Founders Were Gone

It is not unusual for a company dynamic to shift once the founders are gone. Bill Harley and the Davidson brothers were an extraordinarily powerful team. Each one brought unique talents and skills to the mix. They were united in their vision for the company, united in the plans to direct its growth, and united in their response to the challenges of the changing marketplace. They maintained a constant dialogue with their dealers and customers so they could produce the motorcycles that the riders wanted. Their uncanny ability to anticipate customer need was legendary.

Once they were all gone, their special brand of magic went with them. The second-generation managers had been steeped in their brew, but it's only natural that the new soup would have its own distinctive flavor. For the most part, they followed the basic formulas of the founders, except for one. They built tough, reliable machines, and their advertising campaigns were clever and timely. They slipped, however, when it came to listening to their dealers and their customers. The need was clear, yet they were very slow to respond and when they did, the bike was off the mark. By the time they finally struck gold with the Sportster, it was too late to propel them back to the top of the heap. Add on the company's heavy-handed tactics with dealers, and Arthur's carefully nurtured network of loyal team members began to turn into a somewhat dysfunctional family.

Harley-Davidson Was a Union Shop

After Harley became a union shop and William's subsequent death in 1937, the relationship between management and workers began to change. Under William's watch, the tone was more like that of a family, and the interchange of ideas and opinions often resulted in new production methods that made Bill Harley's creations come to life. The reverse was also true. Feedback from the production floor inspired the creative team as they refined existing models and came up with ideas for new ones. After the union contract was signed, that relationship became more adversarial, William's open-door policy virtually evaporated, and there was probably not much of the old-style interaction and teamwork. Perhaps, if there had been, workers would have come up with a good system to easily shift production to the kind of machine needed to meet the British challenge.

Were the British Bikes a Real Threat or Just a Passing Fad?

Harley was the only American motorcycle maker, with a golden reputation both here and abroad. They had never faced a foreign challenge on their own turf, and they had certainly held their own in foreign markets against the same names that began appearing in the United States. Perhaps they felt the Harley name alone was enough to keep the would-be usurpers in their place. Perhaps the company just didn't see the middle-weights catching on the way they did. While it's true that the lopsided tariffs worked against them, you would think that they might have something on the drawing board ready to go in case their appeal to Washington failed. As you know, it did, and seems they didn't have a Plan B.

Looking back, it's easy to pick apart what they did or didn't do or why they were so slow to respond to market demands. Nor can we know what the founders might have done. It was an unprecedented situation.

As the 1950s drew to a close, sales were still in a slump, but not disastrous. Harley was still king of the heavyweights, and its police and commercial accounts were healthy. The British manufacturers had picked up on the American taste for big bikes and began exporting their own 750 cc and 1000 cc models. The British still had the corner of the market for 250 cc and 500 cc middleweights. Even though the Sportster was a rousing success, Harley still had no middleweight motorcycle to round out their line, and no plans to produce one. Instead, it began negotiations to buy into the Italian company Aermacchi so it could import less expensive 250 cc models from Italy to fill the gap. The only new addition on the drawing board in the late 1950s was a little 165 cc runabout scooter called the Topper to challenge the popular Cushman scooter. Harley-Davidson looked forward to the 1960s feeling that it had its bases covered. What it didn't see coming—what nobody saw coming—was that the trickle of Japanese motorcycles coming into the country would become a wave and then a tsunami that would bring the company to its knees.

Timeline for the 1950s

1950   Arthur Davidson and his wife were killed in a car wreck on December 30. The torch was passed to the next generation.

The British motorcycle invasion was in full swing with their 250 cc ad 500 cc bikes making a dent in Harley's market.

1951   The company failed to get Washington to impose a 40 percent tariff on imported motorcycles. Their own overseas sales were suffering from European high tariffs, yet European exporters faced very low U.S. tariffs.

1952   Harley introduced the K model, then the KH, and finally the KHK, all 750 cc machines, styled after the

British bikes. They were no match in speed and performance and sold only moderately well.

1953   Harley celebrated its 50th anniversary.

The KR racing bike began to blow the British away at the racetracks.

Indian folded, leaving Harley as the only American motorcycle manufacturer.

1954   The movie *The Wild One* established the rebel biker image.

The Federal Trade Commission ordered Harley to cease its exclusivity demands on dealers. Harley dealers began stocking British-made motorcycles as well as Harleys.

1956   Elvis Presley appeared on the cover of the May issue of the *Enthusiast* riding his KH.

1957   The Sportster joined the Harley line-up and was an instant success. It was the first of the superbikes.

1958   The Hydra-Glide became the Duo-Glide, a first for both front and rear hydraulic suspensions and rear brakes.

1958–1959   Harley began design and production of the little runabout scooter called the Topper.

Negotiations began to buy into Italian motorcycle maker Aermacchi to import a 250 cc single-cylinder, 4-stroke bike to fill the middleweight niche in the Harley stable.

Chapter 9

The 1960s Rock but Who Rules?

1960 ushered in an era of profound upheaval and change, but for most Americans, things didn't look much different from the late 1950s. Elvis was the King of Rock and Roll, fashion trends hadn't changed much, the economy was good, and the Baby Boomers were heading into high school. The Korean Conflict was long over, and there was only scant mention in the news of some "U.S. military advisors" in Vietnam. The Civil Rights Movement was the biggest single newsmaker, gathering steam by the minute, and about to explode into an unprecedented national movement. For the most part, however, people went about their lives clueless about what would be greeting them down the road as the 1960s unfolded.

Although history books often portray the 1960s as a time of self-indulgence and rebellion and emphasize the sex, drugs, and rock-and-roll image, there was a lot more to it than that. It was a time of tremendous idealism and a new way of looking at the world and human relationships that was different from previous generations. For those of the generation coming of age in the 1960s, it was a time of questioning everything, including our own personal identities and our place in the grand scheme of things. More often than not, the drug use was an attempt to open consciousness, to find answers. The hippie culture changed society in subtle ways that rarely get credit. The biggest, perhaps, was that people from all different backgrounds could live together peacefully and without judgment. Just look at Woodstock! It brought together a half million people for 4 days in a rainy, muddy field, with less than optimum facilities listening to some of the best rock bands in the world, dancing, having fun peacefully and joyfully with no major scuffles and no police in riot gear.

And yes, it was a time of great angst and rebellion, but history often fails to examine why. Could it have been the assassinations of leaders like the Kennedys and Martin Luther King Jr. who had given us hope for a new and better world? A meaningless war that our generation was forced to die in? The brutalization of black people? Read the literature of the times,

and listen closely to the lyrics of the music. You'll understand a little better why that generation became so disillusioned with the status quo and
loudly and clearly challenged it to change.

The seeds planted in those years led to profound changes that we
often take for granted today. Women are able to attend formerly all-male
universities like Harvard, Princeton, and the University of Virginia, to
name only a few. Things like the ongoing quest for self-improvement and
the ability to empathize with those who are suffering or those from different cultures all have their roots in the 1960s. We now have businesses and
organizations that listen to employees and more casual dress in the workplace. We are more open to things like natural healing and have a greater
awareness of the natural world and environmental issues. But let's not
over-idealize the 1960s. There were abuses, of course. But so much good
came out of those times that our country might look very different today
if that turbulent decade had never happened. So, we'll look at Harley's
journey through the 1960s against that backdrop of rapid and often radical change.

1960

The first televised debate between presidential candidates aired
nationwide. Young John F. Kennedy was bright and articulate
and looked great. Rival Richard Nixon looked old and tired and
awkward. Kennedy went on to win the election that November, becoming the youngest U.S. president and the first Catholic
president.

Singers like Joan Baez began the whisperings of the folk music movement, and the song, "We Shall Overcome" became the anthem of
the Civil Rights Movement.

Harley-Davidson greeted the 1960s with what looked like a pretty
good line-up of motorcycles to meet the growing and changing demands
of the marketplace. The Duo-Glide had the heavyweight, touring, and
police segments covered, the Sportster filled the bill for the musclebike
gang, and the 165 cc Hummer was perfect for beginners and casual riders. The 165 also grew to 175 cc with three different versions to suit every
taste. The Pacer was a street bike. The Ranger was the off-road model.
The Scat could accommodate both on- and off-road riders. Harley closed
the deal with Aermacchi to create the European division—Aermacchi
Harley-Davidson—setting the stage for production of the 250 cc and 350 cc
single-cylinder 4-stroke models to challenge the British middleweights
and lightweight bikes from Japan. The little fiberglass runabout Topper
scooter was in production and about to hit the showrooms as well. And,

bless its heart, the three-wheeled Servi-Car was still keeping police and small delivery businesses happy. The company was confident that they had a good, solid base to help them rebuild sagging sales.

To keep costs down, they decided not to build any radically new motorcycles in Milwaukee. They took advantage of low U.S. import tariffs and cheap overseas labor by letting Aermacchi do all the work on the 250s in Italy. All Harley had to do was take delivery off the boat, make sure the logo was on the tank, and deliver them to dealers. Tomahawk Boat Manufacturing Company built the fiberglass bodies for the Toppers. All Harley had to do was drop in the engines and transmissions. They would make only minor changes in the existing models like the Duo-Glide, Hummer, and Sportster that didn't require retooling on the shop floor. New options and accessories—yes. Bold, speculative moves—no. Even with all the company's careful planning, the wild and wooly 1960s had a few surprises in store. Like everybody and everything else, Harley was rocked to the core.

1961

In early May, the Soviet Union sent a man into space for the first time. Following close behind was U.S. astronaut Alan Shepherd aboard Freedom 7.

Physicist Theodore Maiman perfected the laser.

Roger Maris hit his 61st home run, breaking Babe Ruth's single-season home run record.

DOUBLE DILEMMA

After all the foot-dragging in the 1950s, Harley really did have its act together at the beginning of the 1960s in terms of product and marketing strategies. It was confident that it had done its homework about what the customers wanted. Ads were snappy, crisp, and colorful and emphasized the array of bikes to suit every need and taste. They called on potential new riders to "Stand out with a new Harley-Davidson," "Now stay ahead, way ahead with the new Harley-Davidson 250 cc Sprint," and to "Ride the road to real adventure." The KR 750, the racing version of the Sportster, was burning up the racetracks and providing rich fodder for ads aimed at the high performance crowd. In any other times, the old themes of individuality, power and performance, and the freedom of the open road would have been enough to pull in new customers in droves. But not now. Harley was doing everything right, but sales were still sluggish. Why? You'll recognize the answers right away!

DILEMMA 1: THE BAD BOYS BECAME A GENUINE MARKET FORCE

Over the years, more and more motorcycle clubs sprang up around the country, and by the 1960s, membership in the AMA was well over 200,000. Many casual clubs also formed but didn't seek charters from the AMA. That was great news for Harley-Davidson: more potential customers. The ranks of the one percenters also grew, and that was bad news for Harley-Davidson. Most of them rode Harleys and the last thing Harley needed at that point was bad publicity. But they got it anyway.

California was a hot spot, but there were one-percenter clubs just about everywhere. And they were still just that—one percenters. The other 99.9 percent were pretty much just regular folks who loved to ride motorcycles. Unfortunately, they didn't make news. Not too surprising. If you were a journalist looking to get your story published or your photo on the cover of some prominent magazine or your bit of video on the evening news, which would you pick? A happy family off on a couple of Harleys for a picnic in the country with the kids? Or a hairy, tattooed, scary-looking guy on a Harley chopper about to bash another hairy, tattooed, scary-looking guy on a Harley chopper over the head with a beer bottle? They were getting so much coverage that, at times, it seemed like outlaw motorcycle gangs were on the verge of terrorizing the whole country.

As they did after the Hollister incident, the AMA did its best to counter the image. So did Harley-Davidson. Their advertising played up the wholesome image of ordinary folks enjoying the sport of motorcycling. Everyone did everything in their power to repair the damage to the sport in general and Harley in particular. Then, in 1966, Hunter S. Thompson's popular and widely read book *Hell's Angels: The Strange and Terrible Saga of the Outlaw Motorcycle Gangs* pretty much put the icing on the cake. Movies like *Hell's Angels on Wheels* in 1967, with a cameo role by Oakland Hells Angels president Sonny Barger, piled it on thicker. Big Harleys, especially big Harley choppers were synonymous with bad news.

1963

In August, 200,000 peaceful Civil Rights demonstrators gathered at the foot of the Lincoln Memorial in Washington, DC to hear Dr. Martin Luther King's "I Have A Dream" speech.

In November, President Kennedy was assassinated in Dallas, Texas.

President Lyndon Johnson reinstated the military draft to supply more troops to join those already fighting in Vietnam. The antiwar movement started to heat up.

Bob Dylan's song, "The Times They Are a-Changin'," put older Americans on notice that the generation gap was widening.

Peter, Paul, and Mary's rendition of Bob Dylan's "Blowin' in the Wind" became the anthem of the antiwar movement.

Here's the irony of it all. Just like the true one percenters were a tiny minority of motorcyclists, real troublemakers were a tiny minority of the one percenters. But as that tiny minority got more and more publicity, the image got stuck on any guy with long hair, maybe unshaven, wearing a leather jacket and riding a big Harley, even if it wasn't a chopper. True outlaws (make that lawbreakers) and bikers with the outlaw spirit (make that nonconforming individualists) all got lumped together into one category—fearsome and undesirable. Old biker friends have told me there was a time when they weren't welcome at Harley dealerships when they dropped in to see the latest models or get parts for their own bikes. They were told that their presence made other customers "uncomfortable." Harley was clearly losing business because of the media's attention to the troublemakers. Dealers also lost a tremendous amount of business by turning away customers who fit the undesirable "profile" but were no more one percenters than Elvis or Steve McQueen or me, for that matter.

SO WHAT ABOUT THESE CHOPPERS?

Choppers came into full flower in the 1960s, but their origins go further back than you think. The first chopper probably happened the first time somebody took a fender off or rearranged a few things on his bike just to have something different. Tinkerers have been around forever. But the first remakes on any scale started right after World War II.

Soldiers returning from the war, especially those who rode Harleys during their service, kept riding Harleys when they came home. A lot of them bought the surplus bikes the company had on hand after the war. They also had seen the lighter, faster European motorcycles. When they got home, they discovered Harley had nothing to match that. However, they loved

The Captain America Chopper ridden by Peter Fonda in the 1969 movie *Easy Rider*.
Courtesy of the Motorcycle Hall of Fame Museum.

their Harleys and didn't want to buy European bikes, so the answer was to
work on what they had. Most had been trained to work on their machines
during the war, so they had the skills to go as far with it as they wanted.

1964

Congress passed the Civil Rights Act to end racial discrimination.
"Smoking can be hazardous to your health" appeared on cigarette
    packs for the first time.
The Beatles performed in the United States for the first time on the
    Ed Sullivan Show and America was instantly afflicted with Beatle-
    mania. "I Want to Hold Your Hand" was the first of 8 number-one
    singles for the Beatles that year.

Front fenders came off completely. Rear fenders got chopped back
short, with just enough rear tire coverage to keep the rider from getting
splattered with water or mud from the road. They called their new creations "bobbers" after the bobbed rear fenders. Then other things started
to disappear—windshields, big headlights, crash bars, those big comfy
seats. If a part wasn't necessary to the bike's function but made it heavier,
out it went. The result was a lighter, faster machine that also looked cool.

Arlen Ness: Early Trendsetter of Custom Motorcycles

Arlen Ness was a pioneer in the custom bike world. A California boy, he was keen on hot rods but fascinated by the cool low-slung looks of the choppers and drag racing bikes. He wanted one of his own and started saving his semipro bowling winnings until he had the $300 to buy an old 1947 Knucklehead in the late 1960s. Even though he took a lot of grief from his family, he was thrilled and started work on his first chopper.

He did all the work himself, even the paint job. His creation got a lot of attention, and before long he was doing other people's bikes as well. Soon he had so much business that he quit his day job and threw himself full time into customizing. He was making money and building a reputation, but also had a wife and kids to support. He never quite had enough money to buy another bike himself, so he redid the old Knucklehead. In fact, he did it over and over again.

> I kept re-customizing it every year. I'd paint it and fix it up so a magazine could shoot it, then I'd redo it for another magazine.[a]

He discovered early on that there weren't many custom parts available, and he was just getting by on his custom paint jobs. So he started designing some simple custom parts, like handlebars or taking old wheels and getting them chromed. One thing led to another, and he soon found himself doing a booming business in custom parts. The business grew, the parts got wilder, and the mail-order catalogue got bigger. At the same time, he was still building custom choppers inspired by his love for hot rods and dragster bikes.

Nearly 40 years later, Arlen Ness Enterprises is a 70,000-square-foot facility in Dublin, California, featuring a huge showroom with new parts for sale and classic Ness designs of the past on display. He recently opened Arlen Ness Motorcycle Stores in Miami and Daytona as well. By the way, he did finally restore the old Knucklehead to its original 1947 glory, and it holds center stage in the California showroom.

[a]Staff writers, Motorcycle Hall of Fame Museum, "Arlen Ness," http://www.motorcyclemuseum.org/hallofame/hofviopage.asp?id=351 (Last accessed November 30, 2007).

The stripped down bikes continued to evolve through the 1960s and into the 1970s and became known as choppers as more and more things got chopped off or reconfigured. Bikers raked and extended the front forks so the front wheel was further from the bike. Foot pegs closer to the front of the frame replaced the flat plate foot rests. Handlebars got higher—ape hangers. Front tires got thinner, rear tires got fatter and heavy batteries gave way to lightweight magnetos (small alternators that use magnets to generate electricity). Gas tanks got smaller and many bikes sported custom paint jobs or designs unique to that rider.

Most bikers did the work themselves, but as choppers got more popular, more people wanted them. Not everybody was handy with a wrench, and some didn't know the difference between a spark plug and a squirrel, so a whole new world opened up for custom designers and bike builders. All a rider had to do was decide what he or she wanted, and it got built, usually for a hefty price.

It almost got to be a contest to see who could build the wildest bike, and sometimes the designs pushed the envelop of safety. Outrageously long front forks, super high ape hangers, radically low frames and exhaust pipes that reached halfway to the moon prompted some states to pass laws regulating just how far things could go. Most of those laws are still on the books and influence the custom bike market today

DILEMMA 2: THE FOREIGN MOTORCYCLE INVASION GREW AND GREW AND GREW

There was no let up in the flow of British motorcycles into the United States. In fact, they were pouring in. Once the Beatles and other British bands took America by storm, a lot of other things British came along with them—hairstyles, fashions, miniskirts, and an even bigger interest in British bikes. British heavyweights joined the middleweight lineup and cut deeply into one of the foundation lines of Harley's stable. But that wasn't the worst of it.

1965

President Johnson ordered bombing raids on North Vietnam and Americans turned the heat up to fever pitch at antiwar protests all over the country.

The Houston Astrodome opened as the world's first indoor stadium.

Bob Dylan's performance with a rock and roll band at the Newport Folk Festival ushered in the age of folk-rock, signaling a shift from pure folk music to rock.

The Grateful Dead, calling themselves The Warlocks, began performing in San Francisco.

The Japanese wanted to expand their own markets beyond Asia and Europe and had their eye on the United States. They took their time and did their homework well. During the 1950s, representatives from several

Japanese manufacturers toured facilities in Europe, especially Germany. They came to America several times to travel the country, investigate the markets, and visit Harley-Davidson. About this time you might be thinking, "uh oh" and getting a little shiver remembering the Harley plant in Tokyo. It was still in business until 1959, so Japanese manufacturers had immediate access to all the details of Harley design and production. You can bet they took meticulous notes, too. In many ways, Harley-Davidson was the original parent of the Japanese motorcycle industry.

Japanese planners carefully observed every aspect of each of their competitors, including their competition at home in Japan. They saw what worked and what didn't. They spotted even minor flaws in design, parts, and construction that could lead to maintenance or performance problems down the road. Even more important, they studied the market conditions and pinpointed, with amazing accuracy, ways to promote their motorcycles successfully, especially in America.

All the big twins, both Harley and the British brands, were notorious for leaking oil while parked. Riders called it "marking their spot." Japanese makers built crankcases that didn't leak, moving or parked. Harley's carburetor was known to occasionally stick or lose power, so the Japanese "borrowed" some ideas from the British and made their own carburetors smooth and efficient. All the big twins, especially the v-twins, had a vibration problem because of the way they had to be mounted in the frame. The Japanese centered their engines so they were more balanced to cut out the vibration. Their biggest coup, however, was aluminum alloy engines. Harley's engines and parts were cast iron. They were heavy and tended to overheat easily. Even though cast iron is ultimately more durable, aluminum can take more heat and is considerably lighter.

1966

Hunter S. Thompson's book *Hell's Angels: The Strange and Terrible Saga of the Outlaw Motorcycle Gangs* hit the stands.

Yamaha was the first to test the waters in the United States in 1958. It entered one of its air-cooled, two-stroke, single-cylinder bikes in a race in Catalina and did well enough to catch the eye of a lot of riders. Yamaha opened its first dealership in California that same year. By 1960, it was selling bikes through nonexclusive dealers all over the country.

Honda wasn't far behind. In 1959, it created its own dealer network under the banner of the American Honda Motor Company. At that point, it was still just a fledgling company, but it didn't take long for it to rise to the top of the American motorcycle market. The company's first introduction was the Honda Super Cub. The 50 cc 4-stroke overhead valve engine had a top speed of just 40 miles per hour, but it was quiet and smooth, unlike Japanese 2-strokes. It was kind of a combination of scooter and moped and was very user friendly. It was a tough little machine and rarely needed anything other than preventative maintenance like oil changes. It was also less expensive than U.S.-made scooters. Americans fell in love with it. It's still in production today, and more than 30 million of them have been sold worldwide over the years.

Harley Team Racing in the 1960s

The racing version of the Sportster, the KR 750, continued to keep the Harley racing team in the winner's circle through the 1960s. They had a few low moments, and traded championships back and forth with the British and the Japanese. For the most part, though, they remained a bright spot in an otherwise dismal decade.

1960	The top 14 finishers at the Daytona 200 were riding Harley KR 750s.
1961 and 1962	The race belonged to the Brits.
1963	Harley takes the Daytona 200 trophy once again with a KR 750.
1964	Roger Reiman of team Harley brought home the AMA Grand National Championship and the first of back-to-back wins at Daytona with the KR 750.
1965	A Streamliner powered by a 250 cc Sprint racing engine broke land speed records at 177 miles per hour.
	Harley factory rider Bart Markel won the AMA Grand National Dirt Track Championship.
1966	Bart Markel repeated his AMA Grand National Dirt Track Championship win for Harley.
1968	Cal Rayborn won the Daytona 200 with a KR 750.
1969	Cal Rayborn won the Daytona 200 on a KR 750 for the second year in a row.
	Mert Lawill won the AMA Grand National Dirt Track Championship.

Hot on the heels of the Super Cub in 1959 came the 305 cc Dream. It didn't sell well its first year or so, but it would go on to become a foundation bike for Honda. It set the stage for a 10-year domination of the market with such models as the Superhawk and the Scrambler. By 1962 Honda was selling over 40,000 motorcycles a year and had nearly 750 dealers around the country. The secret to their success? A savvy marketing campaign.

We know by now that Harley was having serious image problems. The media had everybody thinking there was an outlaw biker on a Harley behind every bush, and it was taking its toll. Whether by design or by accident, Honda's marketing slogan, launched in 1962, struck a chord with

---

1967

Dr. Christiaan Barnard performed the world's first heart transplant in South Africa.

The first Super Bowl pitted the Green Bay Packers against the Kansas City Chiefs. The Packers won.

Texas Instruments introduced the first hand-held calculator, with a $2,500 price tag.

A new generation of rock music, called acid rock because of its ties to LSD, was introduced at the Monterey Pop Festival. The world got its first good look at Janis Joplin, the Grateful Dead, Jefferson Airplane, Jimi Hendrix, the Byrds, Otis Redding, Ravi Shankar and The Who.

The Doors, with Jim Morrison, released their first album, *The Doors*.

As many as 100,000 young people converged on the Haight-Ashbury neighborhood of San Francisco for what came to be known as the Summer of Love. It was a time of cultural and political rebellion—sex, drugs, and rock and roll. There were gatherings in other cities as well, but San Francisco was the center of the hippie revolution. Hippies were everywhere, and the counterculture spirit moved to front and center in public awareness. Flower children, "make love, not war" bumper stickers, the peace sign, incense, psychedelic colors, communes, and acid rock were the order of the day. Former Harvard professor and LSD researcher/guru, Dr. Timothy Leary, urged a gathering of 30,000 hippies in Golden Gate Park in San Francisco at the first "Human Be-in" to "turn on, tune in, drop out." The phrase became the mantra of the hippie generation.

The Twin Oaks commune was founded in Virginia and is one of the few 1960s communes that's still around today.

The movie, *Hells Angels on Wheels,* hit the theaters. Sonny Barger, founder and president of the Oakland Hells Angels, appeared in the movie.

---

the public and struck gold for the company. "You Meet the Nicest People on A Honda." It was brilliant.

Two years later, Honda became the first foreign advertiser to sponsor the Academy Awards broadcast. After the Super Cub ad aired, Honda was overrun with requests for new dealerships. Other companies approached them about using the Super Cub in ads for their own products. Honda became a force to be reckoned with.

Harley did its best to counter the flow by stepping up ads for the 250 cc Sprint and the Topper scooter. But somehow, ads that headlined "Funsville, USA" and "For a Funderful You in '62" didn't quite get it. Even though sales had been increasing slightly over the years and Harley's commercial and police accounts were, as usual, strong and sound, it lagged far behind Honda in market share and overall sales. For instance: In 1959, Harley's sales were around $16 million. In 1965, $30 million. Honda, on the other hand, went from $500,000 in 1959 to $77 million in 1965 and over $106 million in 1966.[1] Clearly, the bottom was dropping out, and it seemed there was nothing Harley could do to stop it.

DRASTIC MEASURES IN DESPERATE TIMES

Perhaps what was happening at Harley-Davidson was a reflection of the confusion and rebellion of the 1960s. The old ways of doing things weren't cutting it around the country, and it became obvious that the old ways weren't cutting it at Harley either. Sales were nowhere near where they should have been, market share had dropped drastically, and profit margins were razor thin. Harley-Davidson's solution was to open up shares in the company for sale to the public. That's just what they did in 1965 and 1966. Harley and Davidson family members bought up most of the shares.

They used some of the new infusion of cash to tart up the Duo-Glide, added an electric starter, and called it the Electra-Glide. Buyers had the

---

1968

Dr. Martin Luther King was assassinated. Two months later, former U.S. Attorney General and presidential hopeful Robert Kennedy was assassinated.

Under the crush of the Vietnam War, with no end in sight, President Johnson announced that he would not seek reelection.

Shirley Chisholm was America's first African American woman elected to congress.

First Philadelphia Bank installed the first cash dispensing machine now known as the automatic teller machine (ATM).

Aretha Franklin was featured on the cover of *Time* magazine, "Lady Soul Sings It Like It Is."

---

option of either hand or foot gear shift. They felt the foot shift would appeal to newer riders who had been looking at British bikes that already had foot shifts and maybe bring some of the British bike riders over to their side. The old-style hand shift would keep that long-time customer base. The Electra-Glide did not debut to rave reviews, nor was it a great seller at first. Unfortunately, It did little to help Harley's most immediate problems. However, over the next 25 years of its existence, it would become a classic and the unmistakable symbol of the Harley-Davidson Full Dresser.

Things got worse instead of better, and in 1967 the company was in trouble. Here's where the history of what happened next gets a little murky. Some historians say Harley was in such financial trouble that it was facing liquidation and offered the company up for sale. Two large conglomerates stepped up, one being AMF (American Machine and Foundry Company). AMF manufactured leisure-oriented products, like bowling balls and pool

---

The Bright Light of the 1960s: The Arrival of Willie G.

The best thing to happen to Harley-Davidson in the 1960s was the arrival of William G. Davidson, grandson of founder William A., son of company president William H. (young Bill). Known to all as Willie G., he was working as a designer at Ford Motor Company in 1963 when he got the call from his dad to come work for the family company. It was one of the best decisions the company had made in decades because he brought fresh, new ideas and a jolly outlaw spirit that the company desperately needed at the time.

Willie G. might as well have been born on a motorcycle. Harleys were everywhere while he was growing up, and his father rode one to work every day until he left the company in 1973. You know he had more than his share of sidecar rides with his dad as a wee one and then rides behind him in the passenger seat when he was old enough. He was fascinated with racing and started racing and winning in his teens.

He took a graphic arts degree from the University of Wisconsin and went on to study at the Art Center College of Design in Pasadena, California. In California, he ran smack into the world of choppers and custom bikes, and that was it. What he saw and learned there influenced his own designs from then on. Even while he was working at Ford, he was designing and building his own custom bikes in his off hours.

As you might imagine, he locked horns more than once with the older, more conservative folks in the company. Many of them saw his designs as just too wild for Harley, but he hung in there. In 1969, he was promoted to Vice President of Styling, but it would be the early 1970s before any of his designs hit the streets. As future chapters unfold, we'll follow Willie G.'s growing influence on the changing face of Harley-Davidson and his rise to near-iconic status.

---

tables, and seemed inclined to leave Harley's operations intact. The other, Bangor Punta, planned too many radical changes, so the family decided to go with AMF.

Harley-Davidson company historians concede that the company was in deep financial trouble, but they have a slightly different take on the way things came down. They say that once the company opened up shares for public sale, it left them vulnerable to hostile takeover in their weakened condition. And that's just what happened. Rather than fall to a company like Bangor Punta that was making hostile takeover noises and was likely to make radical changes, the company worked out a deal with AMF.

The bottom line was the same. In 1969, the company handed over the reins of authority to AMF. Even though upper-level management and control shifted to AMF as Harley essentially became a subsidiary of the company, Harley's own management team and board of directors stayed on, and operations continued essentially unchanged. It was a bittersweet moment. The company had been saved from almost-certain ruin but was no longer the exclusive kingdom of the Harley and Davidson families.

1969

Apollo 11 landed on the Moon—"That's one small step for man, one giant leap for mankind."

Nearly half a million people converged on Max Yasgur's 600-acre farm in New York for the Woodstock Music Festival, the most famous counterculture event of the 1960s. 32 top rock musicians were there. It lasted four rainy, muddy days—a weekend of music, love, and peace.

Meanwhile, war protests nationwide were at an all-time high. Massive marches and demonstrations were, for the most part, peaceful, though loud. On several occasions, police and National Guard troops were called in "just in case."

The movie Easy Rider, with Peter Fonda, Jack Nicholson, and Dennis Hopper, played to packed theaters.

The Rolling Stones played a concert to thousands at Altamont, California. When a concertgoer approached the stage with a gun, several Hells Angels attacked and stabbed him to death. Even though the event was caught on film and the Angels were acquitted in court, it was another black eye for the outlaw biker image.

All-male universities began admitting women after a panel of three federal judges ruled in favor of a young Virginia woman's sexual discrimination lawsuit against the University of Virginia. Rather than risk lawsuits themselves, they all caved in and began voluntarily admitting women.

YOU HAVE TO WONDER

Even though they were losing the battle with the Japanese bikes and their image had taken a beating thanks to the outlaws, Harley was a very visible brand. In fact, it had reached near-cult status in the custom market. Just about every custom bike or chopper on the streets was a Harley, and the after-market parts and custom businesses were growing by leaps and bounds. When somebody wanted a custom bike, they usually wanted a Harley. Willie G. had seen all of that during his time in Pasadena and was inspired by it. You *know* he must have suggested that they take a strong look at this facet of the market as a direction the company might want to seriously consider. Imagine what might have happened if Harley-Davidson had jumped into the factory custom business early on.

But they didn't. Maybe there just wasn't enough money for that kind of risky speculation even with the stock sales. Maybe management was just too conservative to give it a whirl. Maybe they were so totally repulsed by the outlaw image that they wanted nothing to do with any part of it. Who knows? It's all water under the bridge anyway, and Willie G. would have his day in the not too distant future.

There's a bright side to this whole thing, though. Harley-Davidson found a way to survive, unlike Indian and Excelsior. Even Triumph, BSA, and Norton would fall in future years. But not Harley. It would take a dozen or so years, but the eagle would fly free again and higher than ever.

Timeline for the 1960s

1960   Harley-Davidson introduced the Topper, its first and only scooter, and its first use of fiberglass.

   The Duo-Glide came in four performance levels, three iridescent colors, and a host of options including tinted windshields, saddlebags, and as much chrome as you wanted to slap on it.

   The Sportster had two hot versions, one of them as close to a full-fledged race bike as you could legally get on the street.

1961   Harley debuted the Aermacchi-Harley-Davidson 250 cc Sprint. People weren't nearly as excited about it as they were about the first men in space. Some even went so far as to say if they wanted to buy a Harley, they wanted an American-made one—a *real* Harley.

1962   The 165 Hummer grew to 175 cc with three different versions—the Pacer for the street, the off-road Ranger, and the dual-purpose Scat.

Realizing the potential for using fiberglass in motorcycle production, the company bought a controlling share of the Tomahawk Boat Manufacturing Company.

Feeling they needed to broaden their markets, Harley began producing golf cars, both gas and electric. The first ones were three-wheelers. Four-wheelers came shortly after. By the end of the 1960s, Harley had about a third of the golf car market cornered.

1963   Tomahawk became a fully operational division of Harley-Davidson.

Willie G. Davidson joined the company design department.

1964   The trusty Servi-Car became the first Harley with an electric starter.

1965   The Electra-Glide replaced the Duo-Glide and got an electric starter. So did the Sportster.

1966   Harley introduced the first Shovelhead engines on the Electra-Glide. They got their name because the cylinder covers looked like the working end of a shovel. They replaced the Panhead.

1969   The Sprint engine increased to 350 cc.

Harley-Davidson merged with American Machine and Foundry Company (AMF), essentially ending family ownership of the company.

NOTE

1. Tod Rafferty, *Harley-Davidson: The Ultimate Machine, 100th Anniversary Edition 1903–2003* (Philadelphia, PA: Courage Books, 2002), p. 89.

Chapter 10

The Long Dark Years of the 1970s

The turmoil of the 1960s, especially the country's growing disgust with the Vietnam War, escalated dramatically in 1970. Richard Nixon had been elected president in 1968 on a promise to end the war immediately. It proved a hollow promise, as raids and bombings continued unabated. When the fighting moved into Cambodia, protests all over America exploded in early May, especially on college campuses. People of all stripes and divergent philosophies joined together to burn draft cards and organize massive marches and demonstrations. Police forces began to appear at the protests "just to keep order," but often their presence only served to incite things even further. They represented authority, and authority had proven untrustworthy many times over. President Nixon denounced the protestors as "bums blowing up campuses."

It all came to a head on May 4, 1970 at Kent State University. After three days of occasionally rowdy protests, the Ohio governor overreacted and called in the National Guard to occupy the campus. Nearly 3,000 people gathered on the commons to protest the presence of the Guard and the country's continued presence in Vietnam. What happened next is the great mystery that may never be solved. For some reason, guardsmen began firing into the crowd, killing four students and wounding nine others.

The event sparked a national outrage and demonstrations from coast to coast. 400 colleges and universities voted to strike and shut down in protest. Even at stodgy old William and Mary where I was a student, several departments voted to strike. Most of us boycotted classes and took to the streets in a peaceful but loud demonstration the likes of which Williamsburg had never seen before. 100,000 people marched on Washington. National polls showed most of America felt the war was morally wrong. It was a turning point. It was the beginning of the end of the war. In 1971, the United States began pulling troops out of Vietnam, and by the time the Paris Peace Accords were signed in 1973, the American military presence had all but vanished. The fall of Saigon in 1975 was the final blow. The war was over.

It was also the beginning of the end of Richard Nixon. Suspicion and distrust of the government was at an all-time high, so nobody was surprised when the Watergate scandal broke in 1972 with Nixon at the center of it. Facing impeachment and certain conviction, he resigned in 1974, the only president in history to do so.

Things began to settle down. America was relieved but exhausted, ashamed and disillusioned. So many lives lost or damaged in a senseless war that accomplished nothing. The lies and deceit in the president's fall from grace. All played out on the world stage. But resilient as they are, Americans began to regain their bearings and get on with it. There was a sense of accomplishment, too. They had stood up for what they believed and demanded change. They had ridden the growing wave started in the 1960s and had made a difference. Like the Civil Rights Movement, the antiwar movement had given life to the rallying cry "power to the people."

HARLEY BEGAN A NEW ERA TOO

The mood in Milwaukee probably reflected the mood of the nation but for different reasons. People at Harley-Davidson had to be relieved that the company didn't go down the tubes, but they must have felt a little sad that things ended up the way they did. The company was still taking it on the chin from the smaller, faster, less-expensive Japanese bikes and their market share was still in the basement. On the plus side was hefty financial backing from AMF that would allow them to replace or update outmoded equipment and expand production to move the company forward. They were also happy that the Electra-Glide and the Sportster were still selling well, their police and commercial accounts were still healthy, and Harley golf cars were hugely popular. With the fresh vigor and inspiration of Willie G. and his design crew, Harley was looking forward to the

---

What's a Café Racer?

Café racers have their roots in the 1960s Rocker counterculture in England and can either be the bikes themselves or the people who rode them. The Rockers, and others like them in Europe, were young individualists—rebels—who wanted fast motorcycles to travel from café to café along the twists and turns of country roads. They often played a game called record racing, sending a rider out to a predetermined point as a song was beginning on the jukebox. The challenge for the rider was to get back to the café before the song ended. The bikes could easily hit 100 miles per hour. Café racers had a lot in common with the American choppers, stripped down and customized to suit the unique tastes of the rider. However, the focus was speed and handling rather than cruising and comfort.

---

future. In fact, Willie G. already had new designs ready to go at the end of the 1960s, but everything was put on hold until after the takeover.

In 1970 a new version of the Sportster debuted with styling inspired by the European café racers. It had a fiberglass one piece boat-tail seat/fender combo that stuck out the back like a huge bullet. It got a lot of laughs, but not many sales. People who wanted Sportsters wanted traditional styling. Those who bought them ditched the boat-tail and put on regular seats and fenders. It did give a momentary boost to Harley's aftermarket parts business. The next year, boat-tail was offered as an option in Sparkling Turquoise and Sparkling America (red, white and blue), but there weren't many takers, so the company dropped it in 1972.

You Decide

Time to play "let's pretend" again. You're sitting in on a skull session with Willie G. and the Harley team as they hash over bringing out a new design. The boat-tail pretty much flopped, but the drive to produce something new and dynamic is still alive. At the same time, a lot of the conservative decision makers are still very much a part of the process.

You can no longer ignore the popularity of custom motorcycles. As you've probably noticed, most of them are Harleys, so why shouldn't we be making them ourselves? We also know that our lightweights aren't doing all that well, but our heavier bikes are. Okay, so the boat-tail didn't cut it, but that's probably because we tried it out on an established bike like the Sportster. We've come up with a design for an entirely new motorcycle that would also incorporate the boat-tail. The café racer style is so popular in Europe, it seems like it could catch on here with the right machine. So, here's the idea.

What if we shift our focus off the "traditional" just a little bit and combine elements of the Electra-Glide and the Sportster to create a cruiser with Euro styling? We'll use the 1200 cc engine and frame from the Electra-Glide but add the Sportster front end. We'll modify the boat-tail and add in bold, colorful graphics. The end result would be a chopper-style cruiser with a Euro flare. The comfort, power, and a more contemporary look would appeal to the segment of bikers who want a powerful motorcycle with custom styling. Might go a long way to expanding our customer base.

On the other hand, what if our customers reject the boat-tail again? What if they look at this combination of the two models and reject it as just a mishmash of parts? The Euro bikes are a lot smaller and lighter than 1200 cc, too. It's true that we need something fresh, and we need to acknowledge the success of the custom market. Wouldn't it make more sense, though, to work with a known commodity like the Sportster and do some custom-style modifications there first? You know—test the waters a little bit before we take the plunge with a whole new machine? We need to improve our bottom line and fast. This just seems too risky.

Take a few minutes to mull both sides and make your decision. Read on to see what Harley decided to do.

Harley's Decision

Willie G. and his merry band of visionaries won. In 1971 Harley introduced the FX Super-Glide. The naysayers had their chance at "I told you so" when buyers rejected the red, white, and blue boat-tail once more. *But* they loved the motorcycle. Boat-tails went flying off again, and Harley's aftermarket parts biz got a shot in the arm for a year or so. When the Super-Glide came out again in 1972, minus the boat-tail, looking like an all-American chopper done up Harley style, it was a hit. The bike soon had a loyal following, and became the foundation for the FX line of cruisers for the next 30 years. Through the 1970s and early 1980s, bikes like the Low Rider, Wide Glide, and Sturgis could all claim the Super-Glide as their early ancestor. The Super-Glide put the world on notice that Harley was shifting gears and heading into the factory custom market. Original models with Sparkling America boat-tails are now highly sought-after collector's items.

FX Super-Glide. Courtesy of the Motorcycle Hall of Fame Museum.

THE BLOOM IS OFF THE ROSE

The early 1970s became less and less a time for rejoicing in Milwaukee. The reality of being owned by AMF was starting to sink in. In 1971 AMF replaced president William Davidson (young Bill) with one of its own and moved William to Chairman of the Board. It was the first time since the founding of the company 68 years earlier that a Davidson was not president of the company. In 1973, after repeated disagreements with upper-level AMF management, William resigned and left the company for good. His son, John, was promoted to president. There was still one Harley descendant in a position of authority, but when he died in 1976, that line disappeared from the day-to-day workings of the company.

It was a classic clash of corporate cultures. Before AMF, Harley-Davidson was a traditional family-owned and operated company. They did things their own way in their own time. It was quite different from the bottom-line orientation of AMF. AMF was a huge conglomerate with many divisions, all of which were expected to make money. They didn't have time for the niceties that are perks of a much smaller company.

Worse, they had no feel for motorcycles in general and Harleys in particular. Love of motorcycles and riding had been the heart and soul of Harley-Davidson from the beginning. The founders were riders, as were those who followed them. Many employees and dealers were riders. They loved the sport and they loved Harleys. The AMF folks were polar opposites. They weren't riders. In fact, they didn't seem to give a rip about any of it except as another way to make money. They were viewed as bean counters and suits out for the big bucks.

In 1973 AMF moved all Harley assembly operations to their huge new building in York, Pennsylvania. Other production remained in Milwaukee and components were shipped to York for assembly. The move did nothing to endear AMF with employees in Milwaukee as several hundred of them lost their jobs even though they'd been promised there would be no layoffs. The union promptly called a strike, but there was no turning back. Discontent began to seep down through all levels of the company.

It didn't take the public long to notice the change either. In 1971 the AMF logo appeared on motorcycle tanks alongside the Harley-Davidson logo for the first time. For the long-standing Harley faithful, it was almost heresy. It hammered home the harsh reality that their beloved homegrown family company had been taken over by a multiheaded corporate hydra. Many felt a genuine American icon had been reduced to the level of—dare I say it?—bowling balls. It was worse than shooting a missile into the faces on Mount Rushmore!

PRODUCTION GOES UP, QUALITY GOES DOWN

The infusion of cash from AMF allowed Harley to make some much-needed upgrades and additions to their production facilities and machinery. Before long, greater numbers of motorcycles were coming off the assembly line in record time. Unfortunately, as fast as the motorcycles were going out one door, quality control was going out another. It didn't get better, either. As the flood of Japanese bikes increased, AMF demanded higher production to offset thin profit margins. Honda, in particular, began selling heavyweight cruisers and touring models that seemed to fly out the door as soon as they hit the showroom floors. They were encroaching seriously on Harley's sacred territory. To meet the challenge, Harley came out with a successful 1000 cc version of the Sportster in 1972. It just had to sell a lot of them and all its other models too. So production kept increasing and quality kept sliding.

Part of the problem was having the parts production facilities and final assembly facility 300 miles away from each other, and there was no inventory system. Parts shortages at the assembly plant were common, so employees used substitute parts that weren't always appropriate. Occasionally, parts were left off altogether. The other aspect of the problem was the speed at which the bikes were moving down the assembly line. Even the most conscientious employees simply didn't have time to make sure every nut and bolt was tight enough or every wire connected securely.

Dealers found themselves having to make repairs to brand new bikes right out of the crate before they could even go out on the showroom floor. Harley did provide the parts, but the dealers had to eat the labor costs. They weren't happy at all. A lot of them quit. A lot of them courted any other kind of repair business they could or took part-time jobs elsewhere to keep the doors open. Others just gritted their teeth and hung in, trusting that things would turn around soon.

Customers weren't happy, either. Not only did the Harley name carry the taint of AMF, the bikes were getting a bad reputation for shoddy construction and performance problems. The old timers and the biker crowd with some mechanical skills didn't mind too much. Ever since the first v-twin Harleys hit the street they had been somewhat notorious for niggling little problems like oil leaks, vibration, and carburetors that needed frequent adjusting, so they were used to it. They just fixed what needed fixing and rode. But a lot of new customers actually got to the point of asking dealers if they had any pre-AMF bikes for sale. If they didn't, they lost a sale.

In the mid-1970s AMF took what it hoped would be corrective action. They put Vaughn Beals in charge of Harley operations and Jeffrey Bleustein in charge of engineering and manufacturing. Remember these two names. Beals immediately began making spot checks on all bikes coming off the line before they were crated for shipping. What he found was startling. Nearly every bike he checked had to be sent back to the

Harley Team Racing in the 1970s

The Wrecking Crew felt the effects of the AMF takeover as well. Thin profit margins meant cuts in the racing program. Coupled with some AMA rule changes, the Harley racing team vanished from the American road racing circuit in 1973 but continued to dominate the dirt track. Racing overseas continued until the money ran out. Harley won the European 250 cc class championship from 1974 to 1976, and the 350 cc class championship in 1977, and that was it.

1970 Back home, Harley brought out the XR 750 racing version of the Sportster. It became the bike to beat in the 1970s.

Cal Rayborn broke the world land speed record at the Bonneville Salt Flats in a streamliner with a single Sportster engine at over 265 miles per hour.

1972 The Sportster got a lighter, more powerful aluminum alloy engine. For the next 30 years, the XR 750 was the dominant dirt racing bike.

Mark Brelsford and his XR 750 won the AMA Grand National Championship.

1975 This began a winning streak of four AMA Grand National Championships. Gary Scott won in 1975, and crowd-pleaser Jay Springsteen won the following three years.

line for reworking or repairs. In fact, over 50 percent of the bikes coming off the line failed inspection. Of those that failed, many didn't even have all their parts, due to poor inventory control and parts shortages. In contrast, the Japanese boasted a slim 5 percent failure rate. Making things right was a costly process—thousands and thousands of dollars in parts and labor—at time when profit margins were already thin. It had to be done. Harley's reputation was hanging by a thread.

Bleustein went to work on the engineering and manufacturing department and found it in such disarray that he described it as "an overgrown blacksmith shop."[1] He set a plan into motion to revamp the whole thing over several years. He eventually turned it into an efficient, state-of-the art operation, but it took a while. In the meantime, new Harleys were increasingly the object of ridicule, to put it politely. The running joke among customers was that you had to buy two Harleys—one to ride and the other for parts. Things were so bad that it was not unusual to hear someone make some snide comment like: "Buy a Harley, buy the best. Ride a mile and walk the rest."

IN SPITE OF IT ALL, SALES WERE GOING UP EVERY YEAR

Now, after what you've just read, you'd think that Harleys were so awful that nobody was buying them, but that wasn't the case. Why? There were four major things that worked in Harley's favor and helped build sales in spite of all the problems—some great movies, exquisite advertising, Evel Knievel, and Willie G. Let's take a look at them one by one.

Harley Women in the 1970s: Motorcyclin' Grandma, Hazel Kolb

Hazel spent her early years as a Harley rider, behind her husband, Jack, on long trips around the country. Eventually, she got her own Harley. When Jack died in 1975, Hazel decided to make a memorial ride in his honor all the way around the perimeter of the country. In 1979, at age 53, she set out from Maine.

Harley-Davidson was so enthralled with her story that they backed her in the ride and arranged interviews with the media along the way. Hazel landed on the *Tonight Show* and *Good Morning America,* and a legion of fans grew for the Motorcyclin' Grandma. By the time she finished the ride at the Golden Gate Bridge in San Francisco, she had covered almost 15,000 miles. At a time when the image of motorcycling was suffering, her journey and her story was balm for the soul of the sport. She was a pioneer in making motorcycling a worthy pastime again, especially for women.

She also became the first woman to serve on the AMA Board of Trustees. The AMA Brighter Image Award was renamed for her in the 1990s in honor of her accomplishments and still bears her name today.

Some Great Movies

We've already seen how profoundly movies affected Harley's image in the 1950s and 1960s. There's a saying that even bad publicity is still publicity, and even if it wasn't the kind of publicity Harley wanted at the time, it served a valuable purpose. It kept the Harley-Davidson brand very, very visible. In the early 1970s there were three movies that kept Harley high in the public eye in a much more positive way. All three are classics and did more for the Harley-Davidson brand image of freedom, individuality, and adventure than a multimillion dollar ad campaign ever could.

Easy Rider came out in late 1969 and was still making the rounds of theaters in 1970. Chopped Harleys and the freedom of the open road was the vehicle for the story of three men seeking meaning in their lives. I don't need to tell you the story because you've seen the movie, right? Instead of brawling, trouble-making outlaws, we saw another kind of outlaw—the sensitive, introspective one who turns his back on "the norm" in search of his own truth.

Electra-Glide in Blue ran the tag line: "He's A Good Cop. On A Big Bike. On A Bad Road." The big bike was, of course, a Harley Electra-Glide, and the "bad road" was a cop's journey of bucking the system to find justice. It's a great road movie, full of Harleys, with a theme of honesty, integrity, and the duty to do what's right. Like *Easy Rider,* it depicted the ongoing clash of establishment and the counterculture of the hippie scene as the backdrop for the quest for truth. And yes, the lead character rode a light blue Electra-Glide in some scenes.

It was Bruce Brown's *On Any Sunday,* however, that did the most to elevate the image of motorcycling in general, and Harleys in particular. The movie featured Harley factory racer Mert Lawill and actor Steve Mc-Queen, himself a Harley enthusiast. It was an exciting look at the sport of motorcycling from all angles including the thrill of motorcycle racing. Every time you blinked, there was another Harley on the screen. It was nominated for an Oscar in the documentary category and ranks at the top of the heap in cult-status films. Just as Brown's mid-1960s surfing movie *Endless Summer* had folks running to buy surfboards, *On Any Sunday* had folks heading for the nearest Harley dealer.

Exquisite Advertising

One thing AMF was very good at was advertising. They had a state-of-the-art graphic arts department and the cash to upgrade Harley's lagging capabilities and bankroll a great campaign. The combination of its skill, new tools in Harley's advertising and marketing department, and Harley's knowledge of the product moved Harley ads into a new realm of design and creativity in the 1970s. Long gone were the dorky, almost cartoon-like ads of the 1960s inviting everyone to "Funsville, USA." Slick photography, clever layouts, and hard-hitting, timely copy were the order of the day.

Racing posters in dramatic monotones caught skillful riders laid low in turns or leading the pack in the homestretch on hot XR 750s. Happy couples touring the country on their Electra-Glides were set against panoramas of natural landscapes at sunrise. Another very clever ad used the gas shortages of the 1970s to compare mileage rates of the most popular cars against Harley's mileage. It headlines "America's best economy car . . . isn't a car" and charts the mileage of several makes, the last one a picture of a Harley heralding 48 miles per gallon. One of my favorites is an ad for the Sportster, known for its quick acceleration off the line. Shot in semidarkness, the bike sits alone on a dirt track, dragster starting light pole hidden in shadow in the background, and no copy other than the headline: "Pull the trigger." Powerful!

Ad copy focused on the ongoing relationship between the company and owners long after the sale. New features and options for each model year introduction surrounded carefully shot photos. A small red, white, and blue number 1 was tucked into the corner of each ad with the tag line: "By the people, for the people." It carried the subtle patriotic message that no matter what, Harley was America's number-one and only American-made machine. The biggest headline message, however, pulled hard on the mystique. They finally came out and said it: "The Great American Freedom Machine."

Evel Knievel

In 1971, Harley made the very wise choice of teaming up with daredevil Evel Knievel to provide him with motorcycles and support. His red, white, and blue XR 750 became his trademark bike and brought Harley some of its most powerful publicity. Now you wouldn't think a stuntman could do much for the image of Harley-Davidson, but Evel was no ordinary stuntman. He had this habit of trying to jump his motorcycle over things like the fountains at Caesar's Palace in Las Vegas or 19 cars or 18 Greyhound buses. Sometimes the jumps were successful, but sometimes they weren't, and the crashes were equally spectacular. After ABC's *Wide World of Sports* aired the Caesar's Palace jump, Evel was in demand everywhere. He began performing before thousands of people in places like the Houston Astrodome, and ABC didn't miss a chance to film whatever he was doing for *Wide World of Sports*. In fact, his jumps are among the most-watched ABC programs ever!

With his red, white, and blue cape flying behind him, riding his red, white, and blue Harley, he became a kind of national hero at a time when the country needed one. He traveled the country talking to young people about the importance of abstaining from drugs, living right, and keeping a bright outlook on life. He became a national icon. One of his amazing flying Harleys is part of the collection of the Smithsonian. When he was inducted into the Motorcycle Museum Hall of Fame in 1999, museum director Mark Mederski said, "He lived in a time when motorcycling was looked on askance. When people rooted for him, they were also changing their minds about motorcycles. We don't need that kind of image building now, in part because we had Evel."[2]

Willie G.

Willie G. proved himself to be cast out of the same mold as the founders, especially when it came to going straight to the riding public to find out what they wanted and needed. He started spending less and less time at the office and more and more time at rallies, club gatherings, even swap meets—anywhere riders might gather around the country. He usually rode to them and noticed from the start that he was often the only one there riding a factory stock bike. Just about everything he saw was chopped in some way or other, and many were products of the custom build shops. He talked to everybody he could, asked questions, listened to what they had to say, took notes, and brought the ideas back to the drawing board. Before long clean-cut, short haired, clean-shaven Willie G. had long hair and a beard and had produced the FX Super-Glide, which eventually became a huge seller. He kept riding and he kept listening, and, based on feedback from the public, came out with a line of fairly successful bikes through the 1970s. The FXS Low Rider debuted at Daytona with its dragster handlebars, low-slung seat, forward foot rests, custom exhaust and mag wheels. Hot on its heels was the FXEF Fat Bob with dual gas tanks and bobbed rear fender. Then came his boldest design yet—the XLCR Café Racer. Sportster powered with sleek European styling, it was hot, but the American niche for that kind of bike was just too small to support it, and Harley dropped it after two years. Not only did all these bikes firmly establish Harley as a force in the factory custom market, it established Willie G. as a force to be reckoned with in the design world. Ads for the Café Racer bore the headline: "Only one man could have done this." Soft-spoken, friendly Willie G., with his ready and dazzling smile, became the face of Harley-Davidson. The goodwill he built with current and future riders probably helped sell more Harleys than all the publicity in the world.

Everybody's Hurting Except the Japanese

British bike makers were faring no better than Harley in the Japanese onslaught. The 1960s love affair with all things British had fizzled out, and their sales were suffering as well. Unlike Harley, however, they didn't have the financial backing of a huge conglomerate like AMF. At one point, Triumph, BSA, and Norton banded together under one umbrella to shore each other up, but it was only a temporary fix. By the end of the 1970s, all three companies had pretty much tanked. There were a few revival attempts in the coming years, but nothing that could be sustained. In recent years, the Triumph and Norton brands have resurfaced under new ownership, and it remains to be seen if they ever return to their former glory.

BUT THE NOSEDIVE CONTINUED

There were two things working against the company. First, bikes were still rolling off the assembly line at lightning speed, and quality control was still the pits. Even though sales were increasing every year, costly repairs to bikes fresh off the line were eating into profits. Union workers deeply resented AMF, and there were rumors of deliberate sabotage on the line. Dealers weren't happy, customers weren't happy, and the company had lost many of its core police and commercial accounts.

Second, the flood of well-made, less expensive Japanese bikes was becoming a torrent, and Harley simply couldn't compete with the sheer numbers and low prices. In 1977, AMF and Harley once again went to Washington seeking tariff relief. Once again, they were turned down largely because of dealer testimony. Dealers complained that the company was turning out poor quality bikes, and had yet to come out with a middleweight bike to meet the challenge of the foreign invaders.

After that, AMF had pretty much had it. In 1977, they made Vaughn Beals president and told him to turn the company around or dump it. Beals went straight to work. The perfect opportunity was Harley's upcoming 75th anniversary. Beals and chairman John Davidson organized a cross-country ride with a band of executives to mark the event and try to bolster confidence in the company. They split into two groups and started riding from each coastline, each one taking different routes across the country. Their goal was a meet up at the Louisville races in June 1978. Together, they covered over 37,000 miles, visited hundreds of Harley dealers along the way, and shook a whole lot of hands. It was a masterful PR move. In 1979, Harley had their best sales year ever. But it still wasn't enough, and AMF put the word out that Harley-Davidson was for sale.

Timeline for the 1970s

1970   The street version of the Sportster XR 750 debuted with a red, white, and blue, one-piece fiberglass boat-tail seat/fender combo. The design was a resounding failure.

1971   The Sportster reappeared without the boat-tail and did well.

Willie G.'s FX Super-Glide hit the streets with the same boat-tail assembly as the Sportster and with the same ho-hum reception. It was the first of the custom cruisers inspired by the choppers and custom bike-builders.

Harley joined up with Evel Knievel, providing him with XR 750s for his widely televised jumps.

The AMF logo appeared on Harley tanks for the first time. Harley began producing snowmobiles.

1972   The Super-Glide reappeared minus the boat-tail and was a resounding success.

The 1000 cc Sportster rolled off the line and was a hit.

The FLH Electra-Glide became the first factory-built motorcycle with both front and rear hydraulic brakes.

1973   Motorcycle and golf car assembly operations moved to the new plant in York, Pennsylvania. Several hundred workers in Milwaukee lost their jobs and the union went on strike.

AMF dropped model names in favor of numbers and letters. Boy, did it get hard after that to keep up with which bike was which!

William Davidson (young Bill) left the company.

Sprints got electric starters.

Super-Glides got the teardrop gas tank to make them even sleeker.

1974 The Super-Glides got electric starters.

1975 The company quit making the Sprint.

1976 In honor of the country's bicentennial celebration, Harley put on their own display at Daytona Bike Week called "A Salute to American Motorcycling." They set up their show separately from the main exhibition tent and have continued that tradition ever since.

1977 The company again appealed to Washington for tariff relief in the face of the flood of Japanese heavyweights. Once again, Washington turned them down.

Willie G. presented his dragster-style FXS Low Rider at Daytona. It featured a low-slung seat, dragster handlebars, and distinctive paint job.

Late in the year, Willie G. came out with the Sportster-based Café Racer, but there weren't many takers and the company dropped it the next year.

1978 Company president Vaughn Beals and a convoy of executives began a cross-country ride to celebrate Harley's 75th anniversary. It was also a goodwill ride, as they visited every dealership along the way and met with hundreds of customers and riders.

1979 Harley experienced its best sales year ever. In spite of that, AMF had had enough and put the company up for sale.

Harley introduced the FXEF Fat Bob, named for its big dual gas tanks and bobbed rear fender. It was a smashing success.

NOTES

1. Rich Rovito, "Bleustein Helped Save Harley-Davidson," *The Business Journal of Milwaukee,* Milwaukee, WI, February 22, 2008, http://milwaukee.bizjournals.com/milwaukee/stories/2008/02/25/story12.html?jst=pn_pn_lk.

2. Owen Edwards, "Daredevil," *Smithsonian Magazine,* March 2008, p. 31.

Chapter 11

The Eagle Stretches Its Wings

The 1980s dawned with Harley-Davidson still on the market. A few big companies showed some mild interest, but no offers came. No matter. Vaughn Beals, and a group of 12 other company executives, including Willie G., were putting together a plan and gathering funds to buy Harley-Davidson themselves. Among them were some of the AMF execs, like Jeffrey Bleustein, who had moved over to Harley and ended up falling in love with motorcycling in general and Harley in particular. Bleustein said he decided to jump the AMF ship for Harley for the "opportunity to do something entrepreneurial, to have an equity stake in a company and in fact to be on the side of the underdog. I'd been at Harley-Davidson for six years, and it doesn't take that long to get some of that oil in your blood."[1]

In February 1981, the group issued a letter of intent to buy the company for $81.5 million. Even though everyone from customers to dealers to employees seemed to have harsh feelings toward AMF, Beals was gracious and generous in his comments about his former employer at a news conference announcing the plan.

> From 1969 through 1980, AMF's substantial capital investment in the motorcycle and golf car businesses permitted Harley-Davidson revenues to grow from $49 million to $300 million . . .
>
> AMF helped the Motor Company through a critical stage of growth . . . the most tangible evidence of their success is the company's ability to now stand on its own once again and to look to the future with pride and expectation.[2]

In June it was a done deal. To celebrate, the new owners and a merry band of shareholders set out on a ride from the York, Pennsylvania assembly plant to Milwaukee, with the rallying cry "The Eagle Soars Alone." They stopped at every dealership along the way and met customers and long-time owners to herald the new era at Harley-Davidson. You could almost hear a collective sigh of relief from Harley enthusiasts everywhere!

NEW DIRECTIONS

But 1981 wasn't the greatest time in the world for a buyout. The country was in a recession and interest rates were high. Motorcycle sales in general headed south, something the new Harley-Davidson, Inc. certainly couldn't afford with such a big debt load. It called for drastic measures. Over the next two years the team cut the workforce from top to bottom by 40 percent, cut salaries by 9 percent and froze salaries and wages for two years. They still lost a bundle the first couple of years.

The main focus of the new team was getting Harley quality back on track. That meant they had to look at new ways of doing things companywide and not just on the shop floor. They studied the lean management model of Toyota. They wanted a first-hand look at that style of management in action, so they decided to look at their biggest competitor, Honda. Ironic, don't you think, considering one of the first places Honda visited when the Japanese motorcycle industry was in its infancy was Milwaukee?

When they toured Honda's new Marysville, Ohio, plant in 1981, they were taken aback by what they saw. The assembly area was immaculate, there were very few parts lying around, and the stockrooms had a minimum of parts and supplies, all carefully arranged and documented. The assembly line was humming along, manned by attentive workers at each station. Managers and employees engaged each other freely in design and production discussions, and there was an easy and respectful exchange of information. There was no atmosphere of separation. Quite the reverse. It seemed that everyone, from management to assembly line workers, was recognized as an equal and integral part of the operation. Almost like family. Sound familiar?

Conceding that through their management practices they had become their own worst enemy, the team developed a three-part plan for the York assembly plant. The plan was based on three principles: worker involvement, just-in-time parts manufacturing, and statistical operator control. Let's see how each one went into practice.

Worker Involvement

The first step was to create a plant-wide network of employee groups to get ideas for improving production from the very people involved in the process. Keep in mind that this was a union shop and there was a natural adversarial relationship with management. It took a lot of meetings with the new management and worker reps to ease tensions and understandable skepticism and create a road map for gathering and analyzing information. Once they worked the kinks out and set the plan into practice there was a noticeable shift in the atmosphere in the shop. Workers began to feel valued. The lines of communication were open from top to bottom,

Leadership Portrait—Vaughn Beals

Vaughn Beals, Harley's head for most of the 1980s, was a command/control-style leader. Command/control leadership means that decisions come from the top rather than through ongoing meetings and consensus of the whole organization. Decisions are fast and focus on quick fixes and short-term financial gains. It is especially effective in emergency situations and, skillfully handled, can spark a sustainable turnaround. Rich Teerlink, who followed Beals as president later in the 1980s, said his style was just what Harley-Davidson needed after the buyout.

> When an organization is under extreme pressure—so much so that one wrong move can mean its collapse—authoritarian leadership may very well be necessary. It certainly allows managers to act fast. Vaughn Beals needed speed, and so that's the kind of leadership style he tended to use. Indeed, it came to him quite naturally.[a]

Beals had to make some hard decisions like layoffs and pay cuts and freezes. Before he made his moves, however, he sat down with union leaders and showed them the financial statements. He showed them that the only way the company would survive was to take drastic measures. Nobody liked it, but they all agreed it had to be done. It was a masterful use of the command/control style of management through good communication with staff for the reasons for quick, harsh action. It reduced resistance and ill will, and put the company on stronger financial footing.

He was wise enough to know that his style had its limitations. Once the immediate crisis passed, he softened his position and shifted the focus to a more inclusive mode. He embraced the Japanese management models and worked with the team of 13 buy-out partners to begin a system that would work for Harley-Davidson.

Within five years, the company almost doubled its market share and restored its reputation as a reliable, top-notch motorcycle brand. After the successful IPO (initial public offering), Beals focused more on diversifying the company's holdings and increasing market share.

In 1989, he handed the reins of leadership over to Rich Teerlink but remained chairman of the board until his retirement in 1996.

[a]Rich Teerlink, "Harley's Leadership U-Turn," *Harvard Business Review Online,* http://harvardbusinessonline.hbsp.harvard.edu/hbsp/hbr/articles/article.jsp?articleID=R00411&ml_action=get-article&print=true (Last accessed, November 28, 2007).

and everyone began to feel more and more an important part of the whole. Spirits went up and so did productivity.

Just-in-Time Parts Manufacturing

The second step was a total reorganization of the way the company handled inventory. They adopted a program of inventory control known as MAN—Material As Needed—based on the Toyota Production System that was also used at Honda. Again, communication was the key to monitor the flow of parts and supplies. What do we need and when do we need it? The parts storage areas were tidied up and organized so that everything was visible and accessible and easy to monitor. This step resulted in two very dramatic changes. All the parts needed to put together a motorcycle were on hand at all times and overhead from willy-nilly parts manufacturing and excess inventory went down drastically. The savings from this move alone were quite startling.

Statistical Operator Control

This step began with the line operators themselves. It was aimed at reducing defects and scrap material by reworking motorcycles right on the assembly line. Operators statistically created benchmarks for quality so that workers on the line could easily chart each step of the process. They could assess actual quality against the benchmarks and make improvements when needed right on the spot.

It worked. Quality went up dramatically, much to the relief of their dealers and the hardcore faithful. A new confidence was building in the dealer network and that confidence began to trickle down to customers as well. In 1984 Harley won back the California Highway Patrol contract they had lost years before. For the first time in 10 years, they were able to meet the high standards of police forces again, and those contracts began to grow.

Harley Gets an Image Boost from the Stars

Just as Elvis Presley had given Harley a positive image boost at just the right time, so did celebrities in the 1980s. Photos were popping up everywhere of stars like Mickey Rourke on his custom Harley, Billy Idol on his Springer, Jon Bon Jovi on his own big twin and, of course, the Terminator, Arnold Schwarzenegger. Then there was long-time Harley enthusiast Jay Leno, who rode his Harley on to the set of the *Tonight Show*. There were Harleys in the tabloids, Harleys in fan magazines and Harleys in celebrity publicity shots. Custom Harleys were everywhere in Hollywood. All the money in the world couldn't have bought better advertising.

Harley Women in the 1980s

Becky Brown: Founder of Women in the Wind

In 1973 Becky bought her first Harley—a 1,000 cc XLCH kick-start Sportster. Before long, she turned it into a chopper. She noticed early on that there really weren't many other women riders, so, in the late 1970s, she put a small ad in the local newspaper and was astounded when 10 women responded. They began riding together and came up with the name Women in the Wind. As word got out, more chapters started springing up, and now there are over 60 chapters around the world. She was soon traveling to other countries to ride with members there, touring England and Greece on her Harley. She was the subject of the documentary film *She Lives to Ride* and was featured in the book on women riders *Hear Me Roar: Women, Motorcycles and the Rapture of the Road* by Ann Ferrar.

Women in the Wind became active fundraisers as well. Their yearly Pony Express rides raise money for breast cancer research.

As she and women like Hazel Kolb paved the way for other women riders, the bad girl image began to fade and more women began to ride. Manufacturers began to consider them enough of a market force to design bikes, accessories, and clothing that would suit them better.

Linda "Jo" Giovannoni: Cofounder of Harley Women Magazine

Chicago-born Jo was a gearhead almost from day one. She was fascinated with drag car racing and, when she was old enough, joined a pit crew. When she got her drivers license, she started drag racing herself.

Unfortunately, her first experience with a motorcycle wasn't as much fun. Her boyfriend put her on his old hand-shift-on-the-tank Harley, and after she crashed it a few times, she called it quits. Later, however, he convinced her to try again on a smaller bike, and she loved it.

When she finally got over that first experience with the old Harley, she bought a Sportster. Later, she hooked up with Becky Brown of Women in the Wind and formed the second chapter in Chicago. She started a newsletter for the local chapter and found a lot of women were reading it. She also found there wasn't much else for women bikers to read. "Everything was either very technical or a skin book. That left women enthusiasts in the cold for the most part."[a] A great idea was born.

She and a friend decided to start a magazine for women riders, and in 1985 they went to Milwaukee to see if Harley would back it. Harley was interested in expanding their market with women and gave them a license for three issues, the beginning of *Harley Women*. The magazine took off, and many people credit the magazine with the rapid growth of women riders in the 1990s

[a]Staff writers, "Linda 'Jo' Giovannoni," the Motorcycle Hall of Fame Museum, http://www.motorcyclemuseum.org/halloffame/hofbiopage.asp?id=340 (Last accessed October 17, 2007).

The greatest leap in quality was the 1984 introduction of the 1340 cc Evolution engine. It was more powerful, ran cooler, had less vibration, and didn't leak oil. Eureka! No more "marking your spot." An ad depicting a hot air balloon shaped like a Harley rising above a crowd proclaimed "Thank God They Don't Leak Oil Anymore." Dealers embraced it and so did customers. For the first time, riders didn't have to know anything about working on motorcycle engines. A new generation of nonmechanical, affluent yuppie weekend riders began to join the flock.

The Evolution engine was standard on five models that year including the brand new Softail named for its smooth riding rear shocks. The elegant Softail was styled after Harley classics from the 1940s like the Hydra-Glide, and it was an unqualified hit. The introduction of the new models also signaled a return to naming the bikes instead of just referring to them as letters and numbers. The letters and numbers remained, but the addition of the names gave them Harley "personhood" again, added back a subtle but powerful layer to the mystique, and was a lot less confusing. Things were looking up, and team Harley was feeling pretty darned good about their progress.

SMOOTHING THE BUMPS IN THE ROAD

Things were improving, but it was, by no means, smooth sailing yet. The recession had seriously depressed the market for heavyweight bikes. On top of that, the international market for Japanese bikes was in a slump, so they were dumping their own heavyweights on the market in the United States. Millions of them. In 1982 Harley went to Washington again and this time they were successful. The International Trade Commission issued an antidumping judgment against the Japanese, and President Ronald Reagan slapped a 45 percent, five-year import tariff on heavyweight bikes on top of the existing 4.4 percent. Even though the tariffs would decrease over 5 years, the move bought the company time to for their revitalization plans to work.

Later in 1984, the company hit a couple of big bumps that were almost its undoing. In the years right after the buyout, it had lost around $50 million, in spite of improved sales. That was on top of the debt it already carried from the buyout. Then, Citicorp, which held the note for

Malcolm Forbes

Billionaire publisher Malcolm Forbes did more than his share to raise the sagging image of motorcycling in the 1970s and 1980s. He was quite a character and was in the public eye for a lot more than just *Forbes* magazine. He was an outlaw in is own way. He started riding Harleys in the 1960s and had a New Jersey dealership that grew to be one of the biggest in the country. Over the years, he got plenty of media attention for his worldwide motorcycle trips with Hollywood celebrities like Elizabeth Taylor. He even bought her a Harley—painted lavender to match her eyes. No word if she actually rode it.

He brought new respectability to the sport and showed that riding a Harley was great fun for people from every corner of society. He also made no bones about his dislike for laws regulating motorcyclists. "I think legislative assaults on motorcyclists are totally emotional, disproportionate and totally unfair. . . . They are instigated and implemented by people who know nothing about motorcycling, but have a prejudice. It's easy to curb the freedoms of others when you see no immediate impact on your own."[a]

Before long, lots of business folk and Wall Streeters were sporting leathers and riding Harleys. In 1987, Forbes received the Hazel Kolb Brighter Image Award for all the good will he had generated for the sport.

[a]Staff writers, "Malcolm Forbes," the Motorcycle Hall of Fame Museum, http://www.motorcyclemuseum.org/halloffame/hofbiopage.asp?id=173 (Last accessed September 19, 2007).

the buyout, started making noises about wanting out of the deal. Beals and Chief Financial Officer Richard Teerlink started looking for another lender, but word travels fast in financial circles, and no other banks seemed interested. Things looked grim, and by late 1985 the Harley team started the paperwork to file for Chapter 11 bankruptcy. They even had news releases ready announcing that that were closing down. At the 11th hour, a lender came forward. One of the higher-ups in Heller Financial Corporation was a Harley enthusiast, and Heller agreed to pick up the note. They never regretted it.

Sales continued to climb, and in 1986, Harley scored a profit of over $4 million. Their market share also started to climb. Production costs went down, and the just-in-time inventory system was saving more than $40 million a year. Quality went up, and warranty claims went down. Dealers regained their confidence in the company, lines of communication were open again, and new dealers joined the family. The word was out that Harley was back and getting stronger by the day. Later that year, the company offered 2 million shares of common stock in an IPO on the American Stock Exchange and took in $25 million more than the underwriters had predicted. In 1987 Harley-Davidson, Inc. was officially listed on the New York Stock Exchange (ticker symbol HDI).

They began to diversify operations a little with some of the money raised through stock sales. In 1986, they bought motor home maker Holiday Rambler. That same year, they won a contract from the government to produce military hardware like bomb casings and engines for the drone planes used in target practice.

POLISHING UP THE BRAND IMAGE—ENTER CLYDE FESSLER

In many ways, Clyde Fessler was the Arthur Davidson of the 1970s, 1980s, and 1990s. A skilled marketing and branding strategist, he joined the company in the late 1970s as the Advertising and Promotions Manager, and soon was promoted to Director of Marketing Services. By the time he retired 24 years later, he was Vice President for Business Development.[3]

He came to Harley-Davidson when the company had hit the wall. Quality was at an all-time low, the brand image was tarnished by the undesirable bad boy image, and disheartened dealerships were a mess—both physically and in spirit. He would leave upgrading motorcycle quality to others and set himself to the task of creating a formal branding strategy and transforming the dealerships.

THE BRANDING STRATEGY

During a long skull session with Harley's ad agency, Fessler took a hard look at the differences between Harley-Davidson and the Japanese companies. The Japanese were strong in areas like global marketing thanks to tariff advantages, quick turnaround from drawing board to showroom floor, and long-range planning. Harley's strongest points were a long history, being the only American-made motorcycle, and the Harley mystique. He knew that quality was improving by the day, so that part would take care of itself. He put together a masterful plan to rebuild the brand image and add new layers to the mystique through the 1980s and carry them into the future. Let's take a look at it.

Stick with Tradition

As head of the design department, Willie G. was the man to execute this part of the plan. In his travels to visit dealerships, meet customers, and attend motorcycle functions of all kinds, Willie G. kept hearing the same things. People didn't want Japanese-style bikes or European-style bikes, they wanted old-style Harleys, and they liked the looks of choppers. As you know, Willie G. has a soft spot for the custom bikes himself

Scott Parker leads the pack for yet another Harley victory. From the author's private collection.

and had been adding those touches to his designs for years. He had also learned that deviations from the traditional Harley styling of the earlier years got chilly receptions from the buying public. Just look at the boat-tails and the Café Racer as prime examples. So the road ahead was clear. Stick to the 1940s and 1950s styling and add a touch of the bad boy with custom features.

Play up the American Heritage

Harley was the only American-made motorcycle, and that was fertile ground for adding to the brand image. Profiles showed the typical Harley owner was patriotic, independent-minded, and outdoorsy. Fessler's team came up with the slogan "by the people, for the people." It emphasized the company's heritage, spoke to the patriotism of the typical Harley owner, and drove home the message that Harleys are for everyone, not just bad guys.

Embrace the Outlaw

It was obvious the outlaw biker image was around to stay. Indeed, things like leather jackets and choppers had become almost mainstream. Harley was undoubtedly the symbol of rebellious individualism whether that spirit resided in the heart of a Hells Angel or an accountant or a mom

Harley Team Racing in the 1980s

The Harley team and the XR 750 dominated the dirt tracks in the 1980s.

1980   Randy Goss won the AMA Grand National Championship.

1981   A red letter year for Harley as Scott Parker joined the team. He became the most successful racer in Harley history, with 93 career victories including 9 Grand National Championships in 10 years.

1982   The top three finishers in the Grand National Championships rode Harley XR 750s.

1983   Randy Goss did it again—another Grand National Championship for team Harley.

Jay Springsteen made a one-time return to road racing for the Battle of the Big Twins at Daytona. He easily defeated reigning champ Jimmy Adano, who rode for Ducati.

1989   Scott Parker won the first of his nine Grand National Championships.

You'll notice a gap in years here, but that didn't mean that Harley riders weren't winning. It just meant they didn't accumulate enough points for the championships. Listing all their victories might be another book in itself.

with six kids. The design and styling department had already gotten the green light to continue the retro and custom bike trend, so why not a factory-sponsored "motorcycle gang"? It was actually Vaughn Beals's idea, and in 1983 Fessler created the Harley Owners Group, H.O.G. for short. Anyone who bought a Harley automatically became a member of the group. H.O.G served several purposes.

- It brought thousands of owners back into the company loop and reaffirmed the company's commitment to customer satisfaction after the sale.
- It built upon the camaraderie among owners—in the biker world, the brotherhood. It encouraged the feeling of belonging, and that spirit was attractive to new buyers.
- Through H.O.G.-sponsored events and rallies, the image of the Harley-Davidson motorcycle got a more positive image.

- Through the Fessler-engineered partnership with the Muscular Dystrophy Foundation, H.O.G. sponsored rides to raise money for the charity. It was a far cry from the image of one percenters on their hogs, and was a tremendous boost for Harley's image.

Fessler even used the outlaw image in the company's ad campaigns touting the new level of quality and reliability. An especially masterful ad is a shot of a group of stereotypical, mean-looking bad boy bikers, long hair, beards, tattoos and all, some wearing Harley T-shirts with the headline "Would you sell an unreliable motorcycle to these guys?"

Build a Striking Ad Campaign

The company's ads reflected a new confidence and strength. Taking a page from the founders' playbook, it took a pot shot or two at the competition for copying its designs. A 1983 ad for the new FXRS was a shot of the bike surrounded by Japanese characters with English translations and the headline "Maybe this time nothing will be lost in the translation." Ads hit heavily on themes of individuality and rider loyalty. Ads promoting H.O.G. often featured women riders with the headline "I am Woman. Hear me roar." Another dramatic example is a simple shot of a guy's arm, his body in shadow, his arm emblazoned with an elaborate Harley tattoo and the headline "When was the last time you felt this strongly about anything?"

One of the most expensive advertising moves was the SuperRide promotion, designed to pull in new customers. They ran $3 million worth of television commercials that invited people to visit any Harley dealer in the country to test ride a new bike. Over 40,000 people turned out to ride. Even though the effort didn't produce immediate stellar results, sales did start to go up, and some of the new customers were former owners of Harley competitors.

Extend the Reach

Fessler expanded the clothing and accessories department way beyond the black leather jacket and black T-shirts to appeal to a much wider customer base than the biker crowd. In 1986, Harley MotorClothes offered up everything from jeans to more yuppie-style shirts to baby clothes to women's wear, all emblazoned with the Harley logo. Riders in such togs certainly elevated the image of Harley well above outlaws looking for trouble. There's also something to be said for people from all walks of life wearing Harley T-shirts whether they owned a Harley or not. Great free advertising! Fessler set up outlets in major tourist areas as well as in dealerships. Sales of MotorClothes jumped from $20 million a year to over $100 million in just five years.

The company also began to license the bar and shield logo on a wide range of upscale products. The goal was to give people an opportunity to "feel Harley" even if they didn't own a motorcycle. Fessler's program created such things as the Harley-Davidson Café, Harley Zippo lighters, Harley Christmas ornaments, and Harley children's toys, including a Harley Barbie. The little kids who got a taste of Harley early on might well go on to become the riders of the future. Start them young—very smart thinking! The French make-up giant L'Oreal licensed the logo for a new cologne. Harley-Davidson mall stores began to pop up in the late 1980s and 1990s. Fessler conceded that his only licensing regret was Harley cigarettes.

Upgrade the Dealerships

The next step was cleaning up the image of the dealerships. Most dealers had remained loyal to the company during the hard times, but many had turned into dingy, garage-like hangouts. Fessler worked with the dealers to upgrade facilities, add new lighting to brighten up the showrooms, and required all dealers to add accessories and Motor-Clothes. If they didn't have space, they had to add it on at their own expense. In fact, the expense for all the company-required upgrades came out of dealers' pockets.[4] They weren't thrilled, but they did it. The company made sure they were well stocked with merchandise, including accessories and clothing, along with a good selection of all motorcycle models. The frontline face of Harley-Davidson got a good scrubbing, and it paid off. More and more "mainstreamers" began to visit showrooms and buy motorcycles.

A HAPPY TRIP TO WASHINGTON

Things were going so well that once again, Harley went to Washington, but not to ask for help. This time they went to ask that the tariffs on Japanese heavyweights be lifted—a year before they were due to run out. It was an unprecedented move, and it sent a loud and clear message that Harley was back and better than ever. A few months later, President Reagan visited the York plant to praise the Harley miracle. He toured the plant and chatted with employees. At the end of the tour, he climbed aboard a new Harley just off the line, kick-started it (second try), and revved it up like a true biker.

THE STUFF OF LEGEND

Harley's rise from the ashes has been the subject of more case studies and articles and commentary than almost any other American company. They talk about how a failing company redefined itself completely to become a huge success. They talk about successfully applying the Japanese business models to American manufacturing. But there are a few things I haven't seen get much attention.

1. In the crucial areas of employee and customer involvement, the buyout team of 13, perhaps unknowingly, dipped back into foundational principles of the company that got lost along the way. After Harley became a union shop and William's untimely death two days later, the connection between workers and management dissolved. When those precious lines of communication were cut, it was the end of the ideas and innovations that had come from the shop floor.

   After all the founders were gone, the principle of listening to the riders and customers and meeting their needs went by the wayside. The close ties to dealers weakened. It was painfully obvious beginning in the late 1940s and early 1950s when dealers and customers were screaming for a middleweight Harley and were ignored. Two of the pillars of the company's success crumbled with devastating consequences.

2. The case studies often ignore the loyalty of the hardcore faithful that helped keep Harley going in the worst of times. Even when the quality of the bikes was really awful, they bought them anyway, tinkered with them till they worked right, then went for a ride. Call it the power of the mystique or brand loyalty or whatever you like, but when the going got tough, the bikers were there to keep the ship afloat.

3. Finally, there's the factor of unified vision. Remember that from chapter 2—the power of the dream? After the founders were all dead, the vision became scattered, if it existed at all. When the team of 13 began their new journey, they shared the strong vision of a healthy, thriving company, of Harley once again taking its place on top. Because of the strength of that unified vision and their love for the Harley-Davidson motorcycle, things fell into place in perfect timing to make it all happen. Never doubt the power of the dream.

So, in a way, the resurgence of the company sprang from a return to its roots, even though that return might not have been a conscious one. And what a resurgence it was! From 1986 on, everyone looked forward and upward as Harley sales and profits rose year after year. The eagle was truly free and the coming years would show just how high it could fly.

Timeline for the 1980s

1980   Harley debuted the smooth-riding 1300 cc FLT Tour-Glide with a five-speed transmission and rubber-mounted drivetrain to cut down vibration. It also marked the return of the belt drive, this time Kevlar instead of the leather belts of the early days. Belt drives would become standard on all Harleys within a year or so.

In honor of the Sturgis Motorcycle Rally, Harley introduced the 1300 cc Sturgis model.

1980 was also the year of the Wide-Glide. All three carried the distinctive mark of Willie G.'s custom styling.

1981   13 Harley executives offered a letter of intent to buy the company. The $81.5 million dollar deal was closed in June. There was a celebratory ride from the York plant to Milwaukee with the rallying cry "The Eagle Soars Alone."

1982   With a new operating and management system in place, the quality of motorcycles and production efficiency improved by leaps and bounds. New confidence and innovative ideas led to the release of the Super-Glide II, with its rubber-encased five-speed powertrain, and new upgrades to the Sportster.

1983   In response to the Japanese dumping a million or so heavy-weight bikes in the American marketplace, Harley petitioned Washington for five-year tariff relief and got it.

The company began a series of PR moves to rebuild their image and draw riders and customers back to Harley. The first was the formation of the Harley Owners Group (H.O.G.), with membership open to anyone who bought a Harley. Within a few years, membership grew to nearly 100,000.

SuperRide was another promotion that invited people to test ride a Harley at their nearest dealer. Tens of thousands of people came out for rides after the $3 million TV ad campaign.

1984   Harley released its boldest engine yet—the 1340 cc Evolution. It was fast, ran cooler, and didn't leak oil.

They also introduced the Softail, named for its smooth riding rear shock absorbers.

Harley won the contract to supply motorcycles for the California Highway Patrol. It was a signal that the quality of bikes had improved drastically.

1985   The company headed to the brink of bankruptcy when their lender changed the terms of the buyout financing in 1984. At the last minute, Heller Financial Corporation stepped in to save the day.

1986   Sales climbed, and Harley offered 2 million shares of common stock for sale on the American Stock Exchange. It was the first time that Harley had been publicly traded since the AMF merger.

The whole Sportster line came out with the aluminum-alloy Evolution engine.

The Heritage Softail, with its Evolution engine and 1950s retro styling, debuted with great success.

1987   Harley was approved by the New York Stock Exchange and began trading under the ticker symbol HDI.

Harley petitioned the International Tariff Commission to end the tariffs on heavyweight motorcycles a year early.

The company began the buy-back program for the 883 cc Sportster, offering customers a full-value trade in within two years if they decided to move up to a bigger model.

The company introduced the FLHS Electra Glide Sport, FLSTC Heritage Softail Classic, the FXLR Low Rider Custom and to celebrate the 30th Anniversary of the Sportster, an 1100 cc version of their most popular motorcycle.

1988   Harley celebrated its 85th anniversary with the introduction of the biggest Sportster yet at 1200 cc.

The Springer Softail brought the return of the Springer front forks that had given way to hydraulics with the Hydra-Glide. This time, however, the Springer front end was the product of computer-assisted design and analysis.

Over 60,000 riders celebrated the anniversary at a big bash in Milwaukee.

The Harley-Davidson Traveling Museum began traveling around the country with displays of classic bikes and Harley memorabilia.

1989   Harley left the 1980s in style with a new line of touring bikes. This Ultra Classic line featured a new Tour-Glide and Electra-Glide with cruise control, glove box, four-speaker stereo systems with controls for both rider and passenger, and built-in CB radio.

NOTES

1. Brad Herzog, "The Mild One," *Cornell Alumni Magazine Online,* January/ February 2005, http://cirbellmagazine.cornell.edu/Archive/2005janfebturea/ Feature.html (last accessed October 3, 2007).

2. Thomas Bolfert, *The Big Book of Harley-Davidson.* Official Publication by Harley-Davidson Motor Company. Centennial Edition (Milwaukee, WI: Harley-Davidson, 2002). From a summary on http://www.dtwhog.com/hitory/h1970.htm (last accessed September 10, 2007).

3. Some of the following material on Clyde Fessler's plans was influenced by Glenn Rifkin, "How Harley Davidson Revs Its Brand," *Strategy + Business,* Fourth Quarter, 1997. http://www.strategy-business.com/press/16635507/12878 (last accessed October 18, 2007).

4. Glenn Rifkin, "How Harley Davidson Revs Its Brand," *Strategy + Business,* Fourth Quarter, 1997. http://www.strategy-business.com/press/16635507/12878 (last accessed October 18, 2007).

Chapter 12

The Eagle Flies Higher and Higher and Higher: The 1990s to the Present

Harley-Davidson thundered into 1990 on a road paved with four years of rising sales and profits. The new, more inclusive management style was paying off in high quality motorcycles, more efficient, less costly production, and improved morale company-wide. In the opening days of the 1990s, the company set its sights on product development, expansion in production and marketing, as well as building and refining its fledgling management system into what would become a model program.

FINE TUNING THE MANAGEMENT SYSTEM

Although the company had made great strides toward a smooth relationship with the unions as they worked together to shift the management style, there was still a lot of work to be done. Everyone in the 1980s had been focused on turning the company around, so there was little time to get into more than a basic plan. Given the long years of being wary of one another, it's not surprising that it took some time for company management and union leaders to sit down together and hammer out anything formal.

The new management style in the 1980s was based on the following guidelines. It was a good starting point to build on in the 1990s.

- Management must be totally committed to the Employee Improvement Program to foster mutual trust between employees and management.
- Training in specific problem-solving and quality control techniques is crucial.
- Every employee must feel welcome to take part.
- To show faith, well-trained employees must have responsibility and authority in all aspects of their jobs.
- Employees must work together to help each other learn and grow.

- Employees must focus on solutions to problems, not blaming others.
- Management must continuously encourage learning and intellectual curiosity.[1]

Leadership Portrait: Richard Teerlink

Rich Teerlink joined Harley-Davidson as chief financial officer in 1981, two months after the AMF buyout. He was a member of the committee that developed new operating and financial strategies that helped transform the company from a sinking ship into a profitable enterprise. As bankruptcy was looming in 1985, he engineered the refinancing that saved the day. In 1986, he led the charge of their highly successful entry into the stock market. He took over from Vaughn Beals as president and chief executive officer in 1989.

Teerlink's management style was quite different from Beals's. Whereas Beals was more command/control-oriented, Teerlink was more into sharing power and empowering every employee from the top down.

> Everyone wants to do a great job. It's usually the leaders who get in the way, due to their insecurities or egos. Be aware of controls that are barriers to effectiveness. How do you add value and get people to respect you? Respect them, and they will respect you.[a]

He believed that making money without an ethical foundation and without valuing everyone in the organization was a recipe for trouble. He followed those principles in his own life as well as in his leadership role at Harley-Davidson. His philosophy followed the Harley guiding values—tell the truth, be fair, keep your promises, respect the individual, and encourage intellectual curiosity. "If you are ever driven by money and money alone, you'll make unethical decisions. I've seen it happen. Beware."[b]

Under his watch, he and chief engineer Jeff Bleustein began to refine the management system begun in the 1980s. When he passed the torch to Bleustein in 1997, the company's annual revenues had grown to $1.5 billion with a net income of $143 million. He served as chairman of the board until he retired in 2002.

[a]Rebecca Smith, "An Inside Look at Motorcycle Giant Harley-Davidson," *Update*, 2003, http://www.bus.wisc.edu/update/winter03/harley.asp (Last accessed August 27, 2007).
[b]Ibid.

In the mid-1990s, company president Rich Teerlink, chief engineer Jeff Bleustein, and other executives finally did sit down with the presidents of the two unions, IAM (International Association of Machinists) and PACE (Paper, Allied-Industrial, Chemical and Energy Workers). They came up with a plan they dubbed Partnering. Bleustein, in remarks to the Department of Labor, said the plan had its roots in three key areas:

- The first is that unions are recognized as a valued institution. They're not to be run out of our factories—we're not going to run away from them. They are the legitimate representatives of large numbers of our employees, and we respect their leadership.
- Leadership is shared. Decisions are made jointly. Employees are empowered. They are empowered to make decisions at their work place, because they are the closest to the work and they know what they need in order to get the job done. But also, they are empowered to make decisions and are involved in decisions about other things, such as strategy, new products, and so forth. We are really trying to encourage the best that each of our employees has to give.
- And finally, financial rewards are shared with all employees. Every person at Harley-Davidson is on an incentive program, and the key thing is, it's the same incentive program from everyone—from the factory floor to the executive office, we're all working to the same formula. So when I get a good pay day, so do the people in the factories, so do the people in the accounting department—we all share in it alike.

  Under partnering, we've moved from a traditional labor-management relationship or a hierarchy, to real shared leadership. Many decisions that used to be the exclusive domain of Harley-Davidson management are now open to influence or, in fact, determined jointly with the full participation of our union leaders and the represented employees. . . .

  Our common vision with partnering has become the basis for other collaborative activities including joint visits to our manufacturing suppliers and our retail dealerships. Union members get involved in equipment purchase decisions and there is shared decision-making on difficult issues, such as outsourcing.[2]

The plan was based on a shared vision for the company's success anchored by the company values: tell the truth, be fair, keep your promises, respect the individual and encourage intellectual curiosity. The plan created semiautonomous workgroups, cross-trained in several different areas to increase understanding of processes and fill gaps if there was a shortage of hands in a particular group. Both company management and the unions participated, and the unions were known to call their own on the carpet for shoddy work. Open communication at all levels was key to the success of the workgroups. Union leaders began to share offices with company management, and key management personnel were within earshot of each workgroup. For example, if someone on the shop floor needed help from the engineering department, an engineer was just a few steps away, not six floors up or across the parking lot in another building.

To encourage continuous improvement, the company instituted the incentive programs Bleustein mentioned. The gain-sharing program paid cash incentives company-wide for reaching or exceeding goals for quality, profitability, and product delivery. To ensure that everyone had the opportunity to sharpen their skills, the company began the Harley-Davidson Learning Center in 1995. Employees from the top down could take refresher or upgrade courses in their own area of expertise or specific job-training courses as part of the cross-training program. In 1995 alone, over 2,000 employees signed up for courses. We'll see how this new era of working together played out when the company began to expand operations and facilities and built a new plant in Kansas City, Missouri.

SMASHING NEW MOTORCYCLES WITH AN OLD-TIME FEELING

By 1990, Harley had a lock on the factory custom market with the blend of 1940s and 1950s nostalgia, chopper styling, and modern mechanical updates. It was a dream that Willie G. had been chasing for almost 30 years. In 1990 he brought out his boldest custom design yet—the 1300 cc FLSTF Fat Boy. A 1950s-style adaptation of the popular Heritage Softail, it had high-low shotgun exhausts, disc wheels, flared fenders, metalflake silver paint job, and pigskin seat. There was nothing else like it out there, and it was an instant hit. It began a popular line that continues today. By the way, that was a Fat Boy Arnold Schwarzenegger rode in *Terminator 2*.

Hot on the Fat Boy's heels in 1991 was a five-speed transmission Sportster, much to the delight of riders who wanted a faster, sportier model. The 1,340 cc FXDB Dyna-Glide Sturgis joined the roster, introducing the Dyna line of motorcycles. It was longer and lower, with a chopper-style front end. In black with chrome, it cut an eye-catching, sleek figure on the street. It was also the beginning of a trend of limited edition motorcycles that sold out almost immediately.

The Daytona replaced the Sturgis in the Dyna line in 1992. It, too, was a limited edition of 1,700 to commemorate the 50th Anniversary of Daytona Bike Week. Thanks to the opening of Harley's new $31 million state-of-the-art paint shop that year, the Daytona had the first pearl paint job in black.

To celebrate its 90th anniversary, the company put out two new models, the Dyna Wide-Glide and the limited edition Heritage Softail

1991 Dyna-Glide Sturgis. Courtesy of the Motorcycle Hall of Fame Museum.

Nostalgia. The Wide-Glide put a more custom face on a touring standard, and the rubber-mounted engine and transmission made for a smoother ride. The striking Nostalgia featured a black and white paint job and cowhide for the seat, saddlebags, and passenger back rest. It soon became known as the "Moo Glide" or the "Cow Glide" and was an instant collector's item.

The hits just kept on coming. The 1340 cc Electra Glide Road King debuted in 1994, and its instant popularity was mind-boggling. It was followed in 1995 with the limited edition Electra Glide Ultra Classic to celebrate the bike's 30th anniversary. With its new fuel-injected engine, dual-control stereo system, and CB, it was a Full Dresser hog to die for.

Two new Sportsters hit the streets in 1996—the Custom and the Sport. The Custom featured a 21-inch front wheel, riser handlebars, black paint, and lots of chrome. The Sport was just that—high compression power and rear gas shocks to take the bumps in stride.

By the end of the 1990s, the Touring and Dyna models were sporting the new Twin Cam 88 engine and enough deluxe standard features to make you dizzy. We won't even mention the options! Needless to say, sales were booming and Harley scored year after year of rising sales and profits during the 1990s. It found itself facing an interesting problem—demand was greater than the number of bikes it could produce. Depending on the model or custom options, some buyers waited up to two years before their bikes were delivered. Part of the problem—at least for a while—was that Harley had beefed up their international markets once tariffs were no longer an issue. In 1990, they tripled their international office staff and opened a European parts and accessories warehouse in Germany. By 1992, 30 percent of production, or about 20,000 motorcycles, went overseas. Some dealers at home were a little grumpy about that, saying they had more buyers than bikes.

Even with all the good years of sales, the company was still a little cautious. The domestic bike market was somewhat flat, except for Harley. Knowing that over-optimism had been the company's downfall in the past, management wasn't taking any chances but still increased production by about 10 percent a year. However, the writing was on the wall. They would have to significantly expand their operations and facilities to keep up with rising demand.

GROWING ROOM

On the heels of the new paint facility came a new Parts and Accessories Distribution Center. Consolidating all inventory in one place further refined the just-in-time manufacturing system, making it easier and more efficient to determine what was needed when and where. The new 200,000-square-foot Product Development Center opened in 1997, dedicated to Willie G. That same year, powertrain (engine and transmission) operations expanded and moved to a larger building. As you can see, the company was compartmentalizing and consolidating each aspect of production for more efficiency and better oversight.

Yet Another New Plant

International sales also climbed all through the 1990s, especially in Latin America. In 1998, Harley opened its first assembly plant outside the United States, in Manaus, Brazil.

The biggest project of all was building a new production facility to meet the rapidly rising demand for Harleys. Because of their new partnering agreement with the union, there was never a thought of running off to a nonunion, right-to-work state to build the new facility. Bleustein felt the whole project would be a grand test of their new partnership:

> We wanted to try a whole different way of working together, and set an example for all of our operations. The responsibility for selecting the location was placed in the hands of a committee of three people, a manufacturing executive, and two union representatives. Ultimately, that group made the decision to

build our new plant in Kansas City. That plant opened for business in 1999 . . .

And that plant was founded on the concept that work groups of hourly employees are expected to take the initiative to identify problems and solve them, calling on engineers or other specialists as they feel they need them. No one is allowed to check their brain at the door or to avoid responsibility or accountability for their actions. In planning the factories, these groups of hourly employees, working without supervisors, teamed with engineers to design the entire assembly process and all of the fixtures. And some of the breakthrough concepts they developed are now being reintroduced into our other factories in Pennsylvania and Wisconsin. Hourly employees are also involved in the hiring process. They interview all prospective candidates, make sure they have the requisite skills, and also assure themselves that they are getting real team players.

The executive office for our operations in Kansas City is an example of the mutual respect that exists in that organization. The Harley-Davidson vice president and general manager shares an office with the presidents of the two local unions. In this environment, there are no walls, no partitions, no secrets. The way things are working at our Kansas City operation is just one example of how our people are truly contributing to our success.[3]

It worked. In 1999, the first Sportster rolled off the line at the new 300,000 square foot, $85 million plant. For two years prior, the partnership of management and employees interviewed about 2,000 applicants for 300 jobs before they settled on just the right people with the skills and attitudes to fit in with the new culture. Their efforts paid off. In 1998, *Fortune* magazine named Harley-Davidson as one of the top 100 places to work in the country.

In 1997, Jeff Bleustein took over as president from Rich Teerlink. The following year, the company bought Buell Motorcycle Company and named founder Eric Buell chairman of Buell operations. The move was a savvy bit of market-watching over a number of years. Both Teerlink and Bleustein saw that the younger generations wanted lighter, slimmer bikes with the look and feel of the racers and dragsters. They had learned a good lesson from their predecessors in the late 1950s and 1960s who failed to respond to market demand and nearly cost the company its life. Bleustein said the Buell acquisition was a strategic move to ensure the company's market remained strong. "The key to our future business is to make sure those who are in their prime riding years will find riding relevant and for riding to be one of the things they want to do."[4] The first Buells hit the showrooms in late 1999. The single-cylinder Blast got rave reviews.

Leadership Portrait: Jeffrey Bleustein

In his more than 30 years with Harley-Davidson, Jeff Bleustein went from AMF executive sent in to clean up the engineering department at Harley to vice president for engineering to president and CEO in 1997. In many ways, he was a latter-day Bill Harley. He is a rider himself, and his insights about what makes a good motorcycle and a good ride brought about many positive changes in Harley design and production. Like Bill Harley, quality and reliability were at the top of his list.

He got his first experience with the sorry state of quality in the 1970s when he discovered his brand new Sportster standing in a puddle of oil the morning after he brought it home. That experience led to design changes in the engines that ended the oil leaks and paved the way for the Evolution engine. Other innovations under his watch in engineering included Kevlar belt drives, rubber mounts to cut down on vibration, new suspension systems, and revamping and upgrading the v-twin engine. These improvements were key to Harley's return from near-death.

His leadership style was not only inclusive but invited open communication and a steady flow of ideas through all levels of the company. He was instrumental in expanding the new partnering management system begun in the 1980s and establishing new programs for employee enrichment:

> Our company is stronger if we have 9,000 people thinking each day when they come through the doors of how they can improve things, rather than a dozen or so at the top thinking about it and everyone else waiting to hear from the mountain.[a]

Like Bill Harley, he was always looking to anticipate the customer's wants and needs, especially before the competition did. He read anything he could get his hands on that might give him clues—business journals, news magazines, and travel magazines:

> I'm looking for the "aha" information. I don't want to be the next IBM that didn't pay attention to the personal computer market or Motorola that didn't recognize the change from analog to digital. I don't want to be forced into a comeback mode. . . . I want to read the tea leaves before the tea is ready.[b]

Bleustein handed off to Jim Ziemer in 2005 and is currently the chairman of the board of directors. He owns several Harleys and, of course, works on them himself.

[a]Brad Herzog, "The Mild One," *Cornell Alumni Magazine Online,* Vol. 107, No. 4, January/February 2005, http://cornell-magazine.cornell.edu/Archive/2005janfeb/features/Feature.html (Last accessed September 20, 2007).
[b]Brian Moskal, "Riding High on the Hog," *Expansion Management Online,* June 1, 2004, http://www.expansionmanagement.com/cmd/articledetail/articleid/16129/default.asp (Last accessed July 30, 2007).

Two Great Debuts for Younger Riders

The company timed the introduction of the Buell Blast to coincide with the introduction of the Rider's Edge Academy of Motorcycling. Rider's Edge was aimed at teaching beginning riders the joys of riding, as well as safe and responsible riding. Rider's Edge courses were, and still are, offered through both Harley and Buell dealerships worldwide.

At the end of the 1990s, two other new programs besides Rider's Edge came into being. The first was the Custom Vehicle Operations department to deal solely with the custom motorcycle market. It specializes in lower-volume, high-trim custom bikes. The second was Harley-Davidson Authorized Rentals program. A brilliant diversification move that's still booming today, the program allows riders to rent a late-model Harley while away from home, to try one out before buying one, or just to have some fun. Rentals are available at dealers and authorized nondealers in hundreds of locations around the world. They even provide you with helmets and raingear, a place to stash your luggage if you're traveling, and 24-hour emergency road service.

2000 TO THE PRESENT

Everyone at Harley-Davidson could look back on the 1990s with pride. They'd been a part of one record-breaking year after another in sales, profits, and motorcycles shipped. Each year the numbers rose between 15 and 20 percent over the previous year and were showing no sign of letting up. Stockholders were happy too as they watched their earnings per share grow along with everything else. The amazing yearly consistency inspired Motley Fool writer Bill Barker to title a January 2000 article, "Harley-Davidson: Another Boring Earnings Release."

> For years now, reading the contents of a quarterly report from Harley has been just about the most predictable event that a shareholder can undertake, and last night's earnings release again confirmed that. The report is entitled "Harley-Davidson Reports 14th Consecutive Record Year and Another Record Fourth Quarter," which pretty much sums things up. The rest of the report just sounds like a broken record.[5]

Unfortunately for Mr. Barker, but much to the delight of everyone at Harley-Davidson, there was one boring earnings report after another in the years to come. They did hit a bump in the road in November 2007 after a three-week strike at the York, Pennsylvania, plant, but we'll get to that later. Right now, let's take a look at what they were up to in the beginning years of the new millennium.

Harley Women: 1990s and 2000s

Valerie Thompson, Drag Racer

Valerie's first motorcycle was a 2000 Harley Fat Boy that she rode at her first drag racing event. She was hooked. She went right out and bought a Harley-Davidson V-Rod Destroyer. She went on to set two land speed records, her best at 161.736 miles per hour. Now she has her sights set on breaking her own record, and her goal is to be the first woman to go over 350 miles per hour at the Bonneville Salt Flats. Her next crack at it will be 2009.

Jennifer Snyder: Harley's First Woman Racer

Jennifer was just 17 years old when she was tapped for the Harley racing team at the beginning of the 2001 season. She won her first race at the Formula USA Colonial Downs Pro Singles National Mile in Virginia that same year. She was clearly on her way to the top, but an accident later in her rookie year left her critically injured and out of competition for a year. She returned to the team later and rode for Harley until the end of her contract in 2003.

SHARPENING THE PARTNERING MODEL

The free flow of information through all levels of the company grew, and there was a spirit of "ownership" companywide. Even the most wary of employees became believers as they saw it working from year to year. Production and quality increased, costs went down, and new opportunities for learning and sharing were implemented yearly. Everyone was considered a leader and from that concept came the notion of Leadership Circles (see Figure 12.1).

Imagine three intertwined circles. "Create Demand" encompasses marketing and sales, customer service, design and styling, owners groups like H.O.G., Rider's Edge, the new museum, and archives. "Produce Products" embraces engineering, manufacturing, styling, materials, and cost management and quality control. "Provide Support" includes finance, human resources and legal functions, government affairs, information and communications, planning for the future, and new business development.

Imagine further that the circles overlap deeply into each other to cover the functions and services that are shared by each sector. Each circle has a group of leaders and shifts from one to another depending on what issue is on the table.

At the center of it all is the Leadership and Strategy Council, made up of members from each circle as well as top management from Harley-

Figure 12.1
Leadership Circles

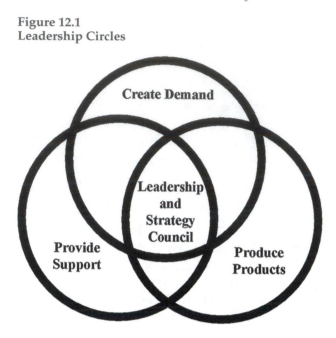

Davidson and Buell Motorcycle Companies, Financial Services, and the Harley-Davidson, Inc. CEO. Armed with information from all the circle leaders, the council forms policy and makes decisions that affect the whole operation. It's plain to see that partnering has become a fine art at Harley, and its success is clearly visible in their increasingly impressive bottom line.

LEARNING CENTERS EXPAND

As the concept of "every employee is a leader" evolved, the Learning Centers evolved too. Harley became a full-blown Learning Organization. Chief learning officer Jim Brolley knows the value of "just-in-time" learning in a company like Harley where balancing work schedules and time for training is like a fine ballet. It must be quick, timely, job-specific, and measurable in terms of the impact on job performance. He reorganized learning programs and introduced some new processes to save time and money, increase productivity, and keep employees engaged and interested. Like everything else at the company, the solutions came through communication with employees and management—through partnering.

- He developed more standardized approaches to learning aimed at specific business or production needs.
- He cut classroom learning time significantly by introducing e-learning programs. The number of courses increased 470 per-

cent, training hours increased by nearly 600 percent, and employees using the system increased almost 250 percent.

- He introduced the concept of blended learning that combines different learning activities including live instructor-led classes, real-time e-learning sessions, and independent study.
- He developed a feedback and evaluation program that included pretraining testing and posttraining evaluation to measure the success of the learning and identify areas for remedial work.
- He created a three-level matrix system for training at all levels. The first level helps employees make the transition to new position or higher level of authority and responsibility. The second level deals with passing on information or suggestions that come "from the top," like seminars or courses, to strengthen the vision and values of the company. The third level focuses on professional development and makes individualized plans for each employee that are reviewed quarterly.
- He published a catalogue of videotapes, books, and courses that employees can check out like library books to make it easier for them to find what they need.[6]

In 2004, the company partnered with two colleges to provide training and degree programs for service technicians. Fort Scott Community College and Pittsburg State University, both in Kansas, provide associate, bachelor, and master's degree programs in applied science and motorcycle service technology and are convenient to the Kansas City plant. Entry-level mechanics can also get training at the Motorcycle Mechanics Institutes in Phoenix, Arizona and Orlando, Florida.

It's All Getting Better Every Year

In 2001, Harley passed Honda in sales for the first time since the 1960s and was named *Forbes* Company of the Year. In 2002, *Industry Week* magazine named Bleustein and Harley-Davidson its Technology Leader of the Year. In 2003, after 18 years of record profits, Bleustein was elected to the World Trade Hall of Fame.

EMBRACING THE OUTLAW—NEW BIKES AND A BOLD MARKETING CAMPAIGN

The Outlaw had become standard at Harley-Davidson by this time. Even the basic models sported custom and chopper features, and Willie G. and his team seemed to be turning out one hit after another. In fact, there were so many of them that listing them here would take all day to read! The highlights of the years are covered in the timeline at the end of the chapter. There's one that's well worth mentioning here, though—the 2000 cc

Softail Deuce. With its twin shotgun exhausts, bobbed rear fender, stretch gas tank with inset instrument panel, and custom handlebars it combined looks with outstanding performance. It became one of the most successful models in Harley history. The company also began grouping their models into categories—Sportster, Dyna, Softail, Touring, and later the VRSC line.

The biggest product events of the early 2000s were the introduction of the Buell line of sporty, racing-style bikes, and the powerful V-Rod, developed on the track as the VR 1000. It made its debut in 2002 and was the first Harley to combine fuel injection and a water-cooled engine for a whopping 115 horsepower.

Hot on the heels of the successful Buell Blast came the Firebolt in 2002 and the Lightning in 2003. They were snapped up immediately by the new generation of young riders looking for speed and racy styling.

Advertising reflected the growing strength and confidence of the company as well. Starting in the 1990s and continuing to the present day, the themes of freedom, individuality, the brotherhood of riders and the outlaw spirit dominated simple but sleek, dramatic ads. Some asked the question "When was the last time you met a stranger and knew he was a brother?" Others proclaimed "The boss's thumb don't reach this far." The boldest, by far, was a 1995 ad for the new Bad Boy. It's a simple, stark photo of an all-black Softail Springer sitting in front of a prison in the middle of nowhere with the simple caption "Just released—the Harley-Davidson Bad Boy." Boy! The company sure had come a long way from the days of distancing themselves as far as possible from the outlaw image. Now it was their bread and butter.

With the coming of the Internet age, Web-based advertising created a new venue to get the word out. Carefully placed banner ads targeted all their market segments. And let's not forget the millions of articles and blogs written about Harley on the Web, complete with photos. You couldn't ask for better free advertising.

For a company of its size, Harley's advertising budget was and still is not all that large, thanks to their exclusive brand licensing program. It is selective, high quality, and designed to keep the company visible worldwide. Today, branding generates well over $1 billion a year. Add to that tremendous sales of clothing and accessories through dealerships and you're talking a lot of revenue and a lot of folks wearing the Harley logo. In 1998 sales totaled $115 million and more than doubled over the next five years.

The power of the Harley brand was unmistakable in 2003 when the company celebrated its 100th anniversary. Over 200,000 bikers converged on Milwaukee for four days of motorcycles, music, and high times. And the parties weren't just in America, either. Worldwide chapters of H.O.G. and other Harley enthusiasts threw parties of their own. Can you think of any other global brand that can claim that kind of brand loyalty?

Harley Team Racing in the 1990s and 2000s

1994   Harley-Davidson returned to professional road racing with the VR 1000 Superbike Race Team. It turned out to be more of a development project than a successful racing effort, even though the VR 1000 performed well. The multimillion dollar project helped refine new technologies like electronic fuel injection and water-cooled engines. The result was the 2002 introduction of the VRSCA V-Rod.

2001   17-year-old Jennifer Snyder became the first woman racer for Harley. An unfortunate accident in her rookie year pretty much ended her career.

2002   Harley launched the Screamin' Eagle/Vance & Hines Pro Stock Motorcycle team to compete in top-level drag racing. Part of the reason for the alliance was to develop a v-twin engine that would be competitive with the four-cylinder engines prevalent in the Pro Stock Motorcycle class.

2003   Andrew Hines started riding for the team, and a V-Rod qualified for each of 15 events on the Pro Stock Motorcycle series. It also made the finals at a couple of events, putting Harley back in Pro Stock contention for the first time since 1980.

VR 1000 race bike that morphed into the highly successful V-Rod. Courtesy of the Motorcycle Hall of Fame Museum.

2004   The team won the NHRA POWERade Pro Stock Motorcycle world championship. 21-year-old Hines won three Pro Stock Motorcycle races, set the national record of 7.016 seconds, and became the youngest professional champion in NHRA history. The team set 13 track E.T. or top-speed records. Hines won the K&N Filters Pro Bike Klash bonus event, the first NHRA title for Harley and the first for a v-twin-powered motorcycle.

2005   Hines won his second consecutive NHRA POWERade Pro Stock Motorcycle championship.

2006   Hines won his third consecutive NHRA POWERade Pro Stock Motorcycle championship, only the third rider in NHRA history to earn three consecutive titles.

2005: A Leadership Change

In 2005, Bleustein handed the reins of the company to Jim Ziemer, and moved to chairman of the board. During Bleustein's tenure, annual revenues grew from $1.5 billion in 1996 to $4.6 billion in 2004, and net income grew from $143 million to $761 million. Stockholders were happy, too. Their equity value shot up more than 400 percent.

By the end of 2006, the company had made $5.8 billion, nearly a 9 percent increase over 2005. U.S. sales were up by nearly 6 percent, and international sales climbed by nearly 19 percent. The company shipped well over 365,000 Harley-Davidson and Buell motorcycles in 2006 and planned to increase that number by 20,000 in 2007. Sales of parts and custom accessories topped $862 million, and general merchandise, like clothing, was over $277 million.[7] But in early February 2007 they hit a little bump in the road.

A New Stock Symbol

In August 2006, Harley changed its stock ticker symbol from HDI to HOG.

THE STRIKE OF 2007

On February 2, 2,800 union workers at the York, Pennsylvania plant went on strike over the company's proposed new wage and benefits plan.

After three weeks, the company and the union reached a compromise, the new contract went into effect, and everybody went back to work. However, the impact of the work stoppage had significant ramifications. Because of the drop in production and subsequent loss of potential income, the company had to lay off 440 employees in Milwaukee, and many of Harley's suppliers had to lay off workers as well during the strike.

With those weeks of lost production, the company downgraded its forecast for motorcycle shipments by 18,000 units for the first quarter of 2007. Depending on how well they could make up the difference during the year, they felt they would still ship 14,000 fewer bikes than planned. By the end of the year, that number turned out to be more like 17,000. Revenues dropped, of course, as did the stock price.

To help reach a balance point, and in the face of predictions of recession in 2008, the company instituted a new dealer allocation program to keep inventories at realistic levels. Instead of dealers getting bikes based on strong sales, they now have to justify their requests with proof of demand. The new plan would roll out over the next year. By shipping only what it can sell, the company may reduce revenues but will protect its brand. It's the brand that allows Harley to make tons of money in the good times and easily get by when things are slower.

Even with the drop in revenues, the company was still hugely profitable. They still had a lock on 50 percent of the U.S. heavyweight bike market. The strike just ended its long winning streak of rising sales and profits.

At the end of 2007, most market analysts felt Harley would be just fine. The company planned on expanding some of its international markets, especially in Latin America and Japan, and had opened its first dealership in mainland China in 2006. *Barron's* writer Vito J. Racanelli puts it well.

> A recession next year probably would delay Harley's recovery—and the stock's achievement of Wall Street's price targets—by a year. But it wouldn't do anything to dent the company's brand appeal among motorcycle riders—and armchair aficionados. When the economic storm passes, look for Harley to hit the gas on revenue and profit growth, and its shares to hit the open road.[8]

Enough said. Let's see where Harley stands today and where it's headed tomorrow.

Timeline for the 1990s and 2000s

1990 Willie G. rolled out his boldest custom bike yet—the FLSTF Fat Boy.

The international offices moved from Connecticut to Milwaukee and the staff tripled. The company also opened a European parts and accessories warehouse in Germany.

1991   Exports had grown from 16 percent in 1987 to 30 percent by 1991. Leading export markets included Canada, West Germany, Japan, and Australia.

A new state-of-the-art paint shop opened in Milwaukee, reflecting the growing demand for custom motorcycles.

The Sportster got a five-speed transmission and the Dyna line debuted with the FXDB Dyna-Glide Sturgis.

1993   Harley bought a small interest in Buell Motorcycles to manufacture sport models using Sportster engines.

The new Dyna Wide-Glide and the FLSTN Heritage Softail Nostalgia appeared in showrooms. The Nostalgia became known as the "Moo Glide" or "Cow Glide" because of all the cowhide accessories.

1994   The classic FLHR Road King debuts to rave reviews.

1995   To celebrate the 30th anniversary of the Electra-Glide, Harley put out the Ultra Classic, the first production bike with fuel injection.

The company began the Harley-Davidson Learning Center.

1996   Two new Sportsters were introduced—the Custom and the Sport.

The Parts and Accessories Distribution Center opened in Milwaukee, further implementing the company's plans for more efficiency and productivity.

A new plant opened in Kansas City, Missouri to help meet the rising demand for motorcycles. The whole process of locating, building, and staffing the plant was carried out under the company's new partnering program.

1997   Jeff Bleustein took over as president from Rich Teerlink. Teerlink became chairman of the board.

1998   A new assembly plant opened in Manaus, Brazil, the first Harley plant outside the United States.

The company bought out Buell Motorcycles.

The Road-Glide replaced the Tour-Glide, with a sleeker look and optional fuel injected engine.

1999   The Touring and Dyna lines got new twin cam 88 engines.

Harley began three new programs—the Custom Vehicle Operations department, the Harley-Davidson Authorized Rentals program, and Rider's Edge.

The Buell Blast hit the showrooms and was an instant hit with the younger, sporty crowd.

2000   The FXSTD Softail Deuce became an instant classic. All 2000 Softail models got the twin cam 88 engine and fuel injected engines.

2002   This was the year of the spectacular VRSCA V-Rod, based on the VR 1000 racer. It was the first bike that combined fuel injection, overhead cams, and a water-cooled engine. It put out 115 horsepower.

The new Buell Firebolt joined the Blast.

2003   The Buell Lightning rounded out the Buell line of sports bikes.

The company celebrated its 100th anniversary in style as more than 200,000 bikers came to the four-day party in Milwaukee. Harley enthusiasts all over the world threw their own parties.

2004   The Sportster line got rubber engine mounts for less vibration, new frames, and bigger rear tires.

The FLHRSI Road King Custom joined the big bike line-up.

2005   The FLSTNI Softail Deluxe and the Springer Softail Classic brought back memories of the 1930s and 1940s with chopper custom features.

Jeff Bleustein passed the torch to Jim Ziemer, and moved over to chairman of the board.

Harley and the Muscular Dystrophy Association celebrated their 25-year partnership.

2006   The Dyna line got six-speed transmissions and the Street Bob joined the family. The Street-Glide joined the Touring line.

Harley opened its first dealership in mainland China.

Harley's stock ticker symbol changed to HOG instead of HDI.

2007   Union workers at the York, Pennsylvania plant called a strike that lasted for over three weeks. It led to layoffs in Milwaukee and the company scaling back its forecasts for motorcycle deliveries and revenues.

NOTES

1. Adapted from Peter C. Reid, *Well Made in America: Lessons from Harley-Davidson on Being the Best* (New York: McGraw-Hill, 1990), p. 163.

2. Remarks by Jeffrey Bleustein, U.S. Department of Labor, Summit on the 21st Century Workforce, 21st Century Workforce Initiative, June 20, 2001, www.do/.gov/21owspeches/jeffrey_bluestein.htm (Last accessed May 28, 2007).

3. Ibid.

4. Brian Moskal, "Riding High on the Hog," *Expansion Management Online*, June 1, 2004, http://www.expansionmanagement.com/cmd/articledetail/articleid/16129/default.as (Last accessed July 30, 2007).

5. Bill Barker, "Harley-Davidson: Another Boring Earnings Release," *The Motley Fool*, January 19, 2000, http://www.fool.com/news/2000/hdi000119.htm (Last accessed November 6, 2007).

6. Adapted from Kellye Whitney, "Action with Attitude: Harley-Davidson's Jim Brolley Revs Up Learning," March 2005, http://www.clomedia.com/departments/2005/February/865/index.php (Last accessed October 19, 2007).

7. Securities and Exchange Commission Form 10-K for Harley-Davidson, Inc., Annual Report, February 27, 2007.

8. Vito J. Racanelli, "Bound for Hog Heaven," *Barron's*, November 26, 2007, http://online.barrons.com/article/SB119586911544902723.html (Last accessed November 28, 2007).

Chapter 13

Harley-Davidson Today and Tomorrow

We fulfill dreams through the experience of motorcycling by providing to motorcyclists and to the general public an expanding line of motorcycles and branded products and services in selected market segments.

Harley-Davidson Mission Statement

In spite of 2007 ending on the first down note since 1986, Harley-Davidson is a flourishing, multibillion dollar, multifaceted company that dominates the U.S. heavyweight motorcycle market. Changes in management style, implementing lean manufacturing just-in-time production practices, and building a learning community of engaged, empowered employees means the company can likely weather the storms that may lie ahead. It is once again like a family working for a common goal. It's looking ahead, it's surveying the landscape, it's planning, and it's ready. Let's take a look at the many faces of Harley-Davidson Incorporated, what each is up to today, and what forces may help shape their future.

Leadership Portrait: Jim Ziemer

Jim Ziemer started working at Harley-Davidson as a freight operator while he was in college. In his 35-plus years with the company, he's passed through just about every nook and cranny of the operation and knows it from top to bottom. He eventually rose to vice president and chief financial officer before he was tapped to take over for Jeff Bleustein in 2005.

He was a key part of the team that set up Partnering and helped build the company into an active learning organization. Most importantly, he's a sound money manager, which is just what the company needs as it faces the economic challenges of the future.

He is an active rider, owns several Harleys, and rides them to work as much as he can.

HARLEY-DAVIDSON TODAY—2008

The Company operates in two segments: the Motorcycles and Related Products and the Financial Services. We'll look at motorcycles first.[1]

Motorcycles and Related Products

This segment includes the group of companies doing business as Harley-Davidson Motor Company and the group of companies doing business as Buell Motorcycle Company. This segment designs, manufactures, and sells at wholesale primarily heavyweight (engine displacement of 651 cc or more) touring, custom, and performance motorcycles. That's pretty obvious. But this segment also includes a line of motorcycle parts, accessories, general merchandise, and related services. Harley is the only major American motorcycle manufacturer and has had the largest share of the U.S. heavyweight motorcycle market since 1986. During 2007, the company's market share was 48.7 percent in the United States. Worldwide motorcycle sales generated about 80 percent of the total net revenue in the motorcycles segment during each year from 2005 through 2007.

There are five families of motorcycles: Touring, Dyna, Softail, Sportster, and VRSC. The first four have air-cooled, 45-degree v-twin engines. The VRSC has a water-cooled, 60-degree v-twin. Engines range in size from 883 cc to 1803 cc.

The 2008 model year includes 31 models of Harley-Davidson heavyweight motorcycles, with suggested retail prices ranging from about $7,000 for a basic Sportster to $23,000 for an Ultra Classic. There are also limited-edition, factory-custom motorcycles through the Custom Vehicle Operation (CVO) program. Motorcycles sold through the CVO program are available in limited quantities and offer unique features, paint schemes,

---

Who Rides a Harley?

The average U.S. rider is a married man in his mid- to late forties with a median household income of approximately $84,300. Nearly two-thirds of U.S. buyers of new Harleys are between the ages of 35 and 54. Nearly three-quarters of the U.S. buyers have at least one year of education beyond high school, and 30 percent have college degrees. About 12 percent of U.S. buyers are women. Three-quarters of Sportster buyers have either previously owned a competitive-brand or are completely new to the sport of motorcycling. The company expects to see Sportster sales lead to sales of its higher-priced models in the future. U.S. buyers of new Harleys have a repurchase intent at or above 80 percent. About 52 percent of those who bought new Harleys had owned one before.[a]

[a] Adapted from Annual Report, Harley-Davidson, Inc. Form 10-K for the Year Ended December 31, 2007, United States Securities and Exchange Commission, February 2007. In the public domain.

---

and accessories. Prices range from $25,000 to a little over $35,000. Dealers have some leeway in setting prices.

Buell emphasizes innovative design, responsive handling, and overall performance. Buell currently offers 10 models, including 8 heavyweight models in its XB line, the 1125R, with a water-cooled engine, and the Blast. The XBs focus on superior handling and are powered by either a 984 cc (XB9) or a 1203 cc (XB12) air-cooled, v-twin engine. XBs run from about $9,000 to $13,000. The 1125R, introduced in 2007, is a high-performance sportbike featuring a water-cooled engine with Buell styling and character. It goes for about $12,000. The Buell Blast is smaller and less expensive than the Buell XB models, with a 492 cc single-cylinder engine. The Blast costs a little under $5,000.

Who Rides a Buell?

The typical age range for a Buell customer is 25 to 55. The average U.S. Buell buyer is a 40-year-old male. The majority of new Buell owners have a median household income of approximately $80,900. About 7 percent are women.[a]

[a] Adapted from Annual Report, Harley-Davidson, Inc. Form 10-K for the Year Ended December 31, 2007, United States Securities and Exchange Commission, February 2007. In the public domain.

The total motorcycle market, including the heavyweights, has four segments:

Standard, which emphasizes simplicity and cost. Sportsters and the Buell Blast have this segment covered.

Performance, which emphasizes handling and acceleration. The Buell XB group and the 1125R fall into this category.

Custom, which emphasizes styling and individual owner customization. The Dyna, Softail, and VRSC motorcycle families as well as a few Sportster models fall under this segment. They feature more retro styling with custom features that have their roots in the choppers of the 1960s and 1970s.

Touring, which emphasizes comfort and amenities for long-distance travel. The company pioneered this segment, which includes the Touring family of bikes with fairings, windshields, and saddlebags or Tour Pak luggage carriers. The 2008 Ultra Classic also features a heated seat and heated handgrips.

Highlights of the 2008 Lines

Harley factory custom design soars to new heights with the Dyna Fat Bob, the Rocker, and the Rocker C. Fourteen models are available in limited-edition 105th anniversary styling and copper and black paint jobs. Antilock braking systems (ABS) are an option on Touring and VRSC models and standard on the Ultra Classic and the Ultra Classic 105th anniversary edition, the CVO Screamin' Eagle Ultra Classic, and the Screamin' Eagle Road King.

What Is the Screamin' Eagle?

If Screamin' Eagle is attached to a bike's name, it indicates high performance—more like a racing machine for the street. It is an outgrowth of the Vance/Hines racing partnership from a few years back. Screamin' Eagle features are not available on all Harley models and are part of Harley's Custom Vehicle Operations (CVO) program.

The Fat Bob sports twin headlights, custom-style exhaust, and a new seat/dragster-style handlebar arrangement for a new riding profile. It looks hot! Take your pick of center-mount or forward foot controls.

The Rocker and Rocker C have a Rockertail one-piece rear end assembly reminiscent of the old hardtails that makes for a smooth ride because the rear tire and fender move together. The word for the Rocker C is "chrome" and lots of it. It also has a cool extra seat that slips under the big seat if you don't have a passenger.

The limited-edition 105th anniversary models are truly breathtaking in copper and black with an anniversary badge and serial number. They're instant collector's items.

All VRSC V-Rods feature a new high-performance, 1250 cc version of the liquid-cooled Revolution v-twin engine, delivering 125 horsepower. ABS is available as a factory option.

The Touring group now features a new Isolated Drive System to cut down on noise and vibration. A new braking system, six-gallon fuel tank, and optional factory-installed cruise control make long distance riding an even greater pleasure.

The CVO group has put out a new Twin Cam 110 in four of the 2008 models—Screamin' Eagle Road King, the Screamin' Eagle Ultra Classic Electra-Glide, the Screamin' Eagle Softail Springer, and the Screamin' Eagle Dyna. The company and CVO have 15 new color combinations and three custom color combinations.

Buell has seven bikes in 2008. The 1125R Superbike is a street/race bike hybrid that delivers power, handling, and agility. It has a new aerodynamic

Corporate Governance

Harley-Davidson, Inc. is governed by a board of directors (eleven members) who come from all areas of industry. They bring diversity of experience and perspective as they maintain company traditions while looking to the future. They meet on a regular basis to review and help set policy and make sure that the company maintains a healthy balance between serving the customer and serving the shareholders. A lot of them ride Harleys, too.

profile and a 1125 cc dual overhead cam, liquid-cooled v-twin Helicon engine that delivers 146 horsepower—huge, but still street-legal.

The Ulysses XB12X combines high performance with the ability to handle dirt and gravel roads as well as the street. It's a true adventure sport bike, with higher, wider handlebars and two-piece windscreen. It's powered by a 103-horsepower Firestorm v-twin. For extra comfort in chilly weather, heated handgrips are standard.

The Buell Ulysses is a high-performance adventure sport motorcycle that is capable of confident travel over dirt, gravel, and other unpaved road surfaces.

The Lightning Series is back, with five models to suit any need or taste. A race-style bike for city driving, the Lightnings feature a middleweight 984 cc v-twin designed to get a quick start at stop lights and easily navigate crazy city traffic.

The entry-level Blast features new styling and great fuel economy—just under 70 mpg. By the way, the Blast is such an easy bike to ride that it's the training bike for the Rider's Edge New Rider course. More than 100,000 riders have gotten their start on a Blast since the program started in 2000.

Clearly, in all segments of the bike business, the innovation continues.

2007 Motorcycle Sales Figures

In 2007, the company shipped 330,619 Harleys. A little over 89,000 of those went to international markets. U.S. shipments were down by over 18,000 bikes, but international shipments were up by a little over 13,000. It shipped 11,513 Buells, all in the United States, down by not quite a thousand.

At the end of 2007, worldwide sales of motorcycles totaled $4.45 billion, down by $106.9 million compared to 2006. International sales accounted for $1.52 billion, up from $1.18 billion the year before. In the United States, sales decreased a little over 6 percent, but international sales went up by over 13 percent. To give some perspective, the entire U.S. heavyweight motorcycle market, not just Harley, was down 5 percent.[a]

[a]Adapted from Annual Report, Harley-Davidson, Inc. Form 10-K for the Year Ended December 31, 2007, United States Securities and Exchange Commission, February 2007. In the public domain.

Related Products

Parts and Accessories covers replacement parts and mechanical and cosmetic accessories. Worldwide income from Parts and Accessories totaled over $800 million for the Motorcycles segment in 2007, a gain of about $6 million over 2006.

General Merchandise includes such things as MotorClothes and other apparel and Harley collectibles. Sales contributed a little over $300 million in worldwide sales in the motorcycles segment in 2007, nearly $28 million more than in 2006.

Licensing

The company's selective licensing program has helped build the brand image. It also brings in a sizeable chunk of income for the motorcycles segment. Licensed products include T-shirts, vehicle and vehicle accessories, jewelry, small leather goods, toys, and numerous other products. There's also a Harley-Davidson café in Las Vegas, Nevada. Although most of the licensing is in the United States, the company continues to expand licensing in the international markets. Royalty revenues from licensing were $46 million, up about $500,000 from the previous year.

Dealerships in 2008

In the United States, the company sells its motorcycles and related products to a network of 684 independently owned full-service Harley-Davidson dealerships. Of these, 307 are combined Harley-Davidson and Buell dealerships. 80 percent of the dealers sell Harleys exclusively. It also sells to the Overseas Military Sales Corporation, which sells to members of the U.S. military. International sales are handled through a network of 685 dealers in Canada, Europe, the Middle East, Japan, East and Southeast Asia, Australia, New Zealand, Latin America, South Africa and, most recently, China. The company is also hoping to open dealerships in India soon.

As you learned in Chapter 12, the company sells motorcycles to U.S. dealers based on an allocation system that changed after sales began to fall in 2007. The new system is more focused on documented anticipated demand in individual markets, rather than solely on previous sales records.

Financial Services

Harley-Davidson Financial Services (HDFS) operates under the trade name Harley-Davidson Credit and provides wholesale financial services to Harley-Davidson and Buell dealers and retail financing to buyers. HDFS also includes Harley-Davidson Insurance, offering motorcycle insurance policies, extended service contracts, gap coverage, and debt protection for the folks who buy bikes.

Dealers can finance upgrades to their buildings and facilities, motorcycles, and parts and accessories. In 2007, over 90 percent of dealers in the United States, Canada, and Europe took advantage of the service.

Consumer lending services include installment buying for new and used Harley-Davidson and Buell motorcycles. Financial services are available through most Harley-Davidson and Buell dealers in the United States and Canada. Insurance services are also available to customers through dealers in the United States and Canada.

In 2007, HDFS operating income was $212.2 million. That's a slim but welcome increase over last year's $210.7 million.[2]

HARLEY-DAVIDSON PHILANTHROPY

Like the original founders, the company today supports the good work of many groups through its alliance with the Muscular Dystrophy Association (MDA) and through the Harley-Davidson Foundation.

Harley hooked up with MDA in 1980. Since then, through fundraising events run through dealers, H.O.G., and corporate headquarters, they have raised more than $65 million dollars for research and to support both children and adults with muscular dystrophy.

H.O.G. Today

Today, the Harley Owners Group has over a million members worldwide. It is the largest factory-sponsored motorcycle club in the world. They sponsor fund-raising events, rallies, and rides, and are a big part of the company anniversary celebrations in Milwaukee.

The Harley-Davidson Foundation is nonprofit foundation set up to support the communities where their facilities are located. The foundation awards grants to community-based projects in education, the arts, health, and environmental areas aimed at improving the quality of life. It also supports a few national programs, especially those for veterans.

CHALLENGES FACING THE COMPANY TODAY AND TOMORROW

Lawsuits

It would be a rare day, indeed, to find a company as large as Harley that wasn't facing a few lawsuits of one kind or another. Harley has a few to contend with, and resolution could take years.[3]

- Several shareholder lawsuits.
- A security breach lawsuit after a company laptop that had confidential customer information on it was lost.
- A cam bearing lawsuit alleging the part was defective, even though Harley had extended the warranty on the parts significantly.
- Various and sundry product liability suits for which they have insurance.

Environmental Cleanup

When the 13 executives bought out the company from AMF, they got the York, Pennsylvania, plant in the deal. What they didn't know they were getting was the environmental issues that went with it. The facility had been used by the Navy, then by AMF. Soil and groundwater contamination turned up later, and the company has been working with the EPA over the years to make things right. The Navy agreed to help share the cost, and it contributes to a trust fund set up to help pay for the cleanup. The company also contributes its share. It is an ongoing process and not expected to be complete until 2012. Unless something unforeseen comes up, the company appears to have the money socked away to cover everything. Some of their clean-up efforts had to be done over, so there could be added expense in the coming years.[4]

Harley-Davidson's Corporate Environmental Policy

Just as every employee is a partner in the business end of things at Harley-Davidson, they are also expected to be conscientious about their role in protecting the environment. That means everybody from the top down. To that end, the company has set guidelines that include:

- Training about sound environmental practices.
- In-house recycling of materials and water as much as possible before disposal.
- Open communication and monitoring for responsible, energy-efficient operating practices and compliance with environmental regulations.
- Ensuring that operating practices meet environmental regulations wherever the company does business.
- Making the company's position on environmental quality known to all.[a]

[a]Adapted from "Corporate Environmental Policy," Harley-Davidson, Inc., February 2006.

The Custom Motorcycle Market

You've probably seen them. Brad Pitt on his Indian Larry Legacy bike, a reported $70,000 birthday present from Angelina Jolie. Or maybe you've seen the Milwaukee Iron Bike Build on the Discovery Channel. Or maybe some of the high-ticket customs from Jesse James's West Coast Choppers. Custom motorcycle shops are popping up all over the country, and custom-built bikes are all the rage among celebrities who pay tens of thousands of dollars for a one-off bike built from the ground up. Not all of the bikes are as expensive as Brad Pitt's, and more mainstream folks are

Milwaukee Iron built this custom bike named KarnEvil for the Discovery Channel as the first part of a series on custom bike building. Courtesy of Randy Simpson at Milwaukee Iron. In memory of Gary Woodford. Copyright Milwaukee Iron Inc.

buying them from some of the less expensive builders. The custom bike business is becoming a strong force in the marketplace.

These bikes begin from nothing but sheet metal, raw tubing, and a design. The frames, handlebars, tanks, and often the exhausts are made from scratch. Engines come from other sources, but for the most part, the bikes are almost all handmade. Their inspiration has fueled a robust after-market parts segment of motorcycle sales as well. Remember Arlen Ness?

The Virginia Tech Victory Bike Build—Doing Good Wherever You Can

Bikers can be a caring bunch. After watching the tragic shooting unfold at Virginia Tech in April 2007 that left 33 students dead, custom bike builders Milwaukee Iron in Lynchburg, Virginia, and Milwaukee Iron 2 in Myrtle Beach, South Carolina, knew that they had to do something to make a difference. So they set out to build a commemorative bike to be auctioned off to benefit the Memorial Scholarship Fund. As word started to get around, donations of parts and cash started to pour in. Dirty South Choppers in Palmyra, Virginia donated the frame, and Virginia jeweler Charles Kingrea designed and made a ring to go with the bike. The bike sports Virginia Tech colors and will be auctioned in October 2008 with the hope that it will bring up to $100,000 for the fund.

We know that Harley is not likely to get into the one-of-a-kind motorcycle business. But we also know that Willie G. keeps a close eye on the custom market trend. So it just remains to be seen how this market will affect future sales.

The Economy

Depending on which commentator you listen to, we're either entering a recession or already in one in 2008. Since motorcycles are luxury items for most people, the market can take a hit if a recession comes along, a big hit if it deepens or goes on for a long time. In the last 20 years, the company has weathered a few of them successfully and it seems well-positioned to do the same this time around. CEO Jim Ziemer says the company is ready for whatever the economy may throw at it:

> Harley-Davidson managed through a weak U.S. economy during 2007. . . . While these are challenging times in the U.S., our international dealer network delivered double digit retail sales growth in the fourth quarter and for the full year of 2007. We expect the U.S. economy to continue to be very challenging in 2008, and we will closely monitor the retail environment and regularly assess our wholesale shipments throughout the year.[5]

Aging Core Rider Group

The baby boomers are getting older. They also form the core group of buyers for Harleys. What's going to happen when they're just too old to hold up a big hog? Some of them have suggested that Harley consider trikes, like the great-looking chopper trikes of the 1960s and 1970s. A lot of the biker crowd think these might be just the thing for the octogenarian bikers of the future. One thing the company has learned over the years is to not ignore any segment of the market, and this is a big one, so who knows. Maybe Willie G. has something up his sleeve.

There will always be a core group of riders about the age the baby boomers are now. It may not be as large a group, so the company is making sure it has its bases covered in younger markets as well.

Former President Jeff Bleustein says, "we don't ever want to alienate them, but at the same time we want to reach out to new groups of customers—people who aren't yet in the family. There are a lot more years in those baby boomers, but we're also looking to the next several generations and making sure we're relevant to them."[6]

SO, HERE WE ARE

We've come to the end of our journey with Harley-Davidson, at least for now. The company is changing and shifting and growing and looking to the future. Willie G. shows no end to the depth of his creativity, and beautiful, powerful, tough motorcycles keep rolling off the line.

As the company celebrates its 105th anniversary this year, the Harley folks will have millions of enthusiasts around the world celebrating with them, even if they don't own a Harley. Milwaukee will be mayhem in August with a half-million bikers expected for the biggest Harley anniversary party ever featuring motorcycles, great food, great parties, top-notch musicians headlined by Bruce Springsteen, and the opening of the new Harley-Davidson Museum.

Harley has come a long way, sometimes over a hard road, and it has a lot to be proud of. I'm quite sure that Bill and Arthur and Walter and William would be totally overjoyed to see how far their little born-in-a-basement business has come.

Now it's time to ride. So come on, outlaws. Light those fires, even if they're only in your head, and keep the shiny side up.

NOTES

1. Much of the material in this chapter has been adapted from Securities and Exchange Commission Form 10-K for Harley-Davidson, Inc., Annual Report, February 27, 2007. In the public domain.

2. Ibid.

3. Ibid.

4. Ibid.

5. Press Release, "Harley-Davidson Reports Fourth Quarter and Full Year Results for 2007, Milwaukee, Wis.," January 25, 2008, http://investor.harley-davidson.com/ReleaseDetail.cfm?ReleaseID=289615&bmLocale=en_US (last accessed February 1, 2008).

6. Brad Herzog, "The Mild One," *Cornell Alumni Magazine Online,* January/February 2005, Vol. 107, No. 4, http://cornell-magazine.cornell.edu/Archive/2005janfeb/features/Feature.html (last accessed September 27, 2007).

Appendix A

Harley-Davidson Timeline

Late 1880s–1901 Some European companies were already producing motorized bicycles. A couple of American companies like Indian and Excelsior were producing quality bikes for the enthusiast market. A few smaller companies were making cheap imitations that didn't hold up.

Bill and Arthur knew about them, and became determined to build their own, only better.

1900–1901 Sometime during this period, Bill and Arthur were given the plans for the DeDion engine.

1901–1903 Bill and Arthur began making parts based on the DeDion plans but realized they needed more skilled mechanical help, so they conned Walter into joining the company.

With Walter's help, they built their first motorized bicycle. It proved to be underpowered, with a weak frame, so it was totally redesigned.

1903 They moved their operation into the backyard workshop built for them by the Davidson's Dad.

Testing of the new model was successful, and they produced their first three bikes, all presold.

Bill Harley went off to engineering school at the University of Wisconsin, while production continued at home.

This was a banner year for transportation. Bill, Arthur and Walter sold their first official Harley-Davidson motorcycles, Henry Ford introduced the Model A Ford automobile, and the Wright Brothers made the first manned flight at Kitty Hawk, North Carolina.

1904   The Motor Company produced eight motorcycles and the first dealership opened in Chicago, Illinois.

1905   Building began on a new factory on Juneau Avenue.

1906   The company moved into the new factory, hired six more employees, and started producing about one motorcycle a week. Arthur put together the first catalogue, and the Silent Grey Fellow made its debut with a bigger engine and a new front-end suspension. The Springer front end would be the standard for the next 40 years.

1907   Arthur and Walter left their day jobs to focus their attention fully on their growing company. William quit his job with the railroad and joined them. Factory size doubled and they hired on 18 more workers. Production tripled to 150 motorcycles that year.

The company became a corporation that year, with Walter as president, Bill the chief engineer and treasurer, Arthur the sales manager and secretary, and William vice president and works manager. The stock was divided evenly among them.

Arthur began recruiting dealers in earnest. He focused on bicycle dealers with showrooms and salespeople and easy rail access for shipping to more distant locations. He began building his ad campaign at the same time, touting their bikes' strength, durability, and racing performance under private owner/riders.

1908   The company made its first official entry into racing when Walter entered and won the FAM Endurance Run with a perfect score. At the same time, he set an FAM record for fuel economy at 188.234 miles per gallon. As word of Walter's victory on the factory-stock Silent Grey Fellow spread, sales increased dramatically.

The Detroit Police Department took delivery of the first motorcycles for police duty, and traded in their horses for Harleys.

Bill Harley graduated from engineering school and returned to the company full-time late in the year.

1909   Harley-Davidson put out its first v-twin powered motorcycle.

1910   The company used the "Bar and Shield" logo for the first time and trademarked it a year later.

Privately owned Harleys had begun to make a big mark in the racing scene.

1911   The new and improved v-twin reappeared and was a success. The new F-head engine becomes stock on all Harleys until 1929. Other improvements included a chain drive, clutch, and the more comfortable Ful-Floteing seat.

1912   There were 200 Harley dealers nationwide, and the first sales outside the United States began with shipments to Japan.

Construction began on a new six-story factory/corporate headquarters building on the Juneau Avenue site.

The company put out its first spare parts catalogue and set up a new department just for parts and accessories.

1913   The company finally decided that a racing team would be to its advantage, so Bill Harley formed the Racing Department with William Ottaway as his assistant.

By the end of the year, the company had sold nearly 13,000 motorcycles.

The Forecar Delivery Van entered service for commercial markets.

1914   The company fielded its first racing team, which wasted no time in dominating the sport and picking up the nickname "The Wrecking Crew."

F-head singles and v-twins got new clutch and brake pedals, as well as headlights.

Sidecars made their successful debut.

1915   Harley motorcycles get 3-speed transmissions and a passenger seat.

Avis and Effie Hotchkiss were the first women to ride coast to coast on a motorcycle.

1916   The company began publishing the *Enthusiast* magazine, which is still in publication today.

Sales were solid—about 5,000 motorcycles a year.

1917   The company geared up to produce motorcycles and sidecars for the military during World War I. About one-third of that year's production was sold for the war effort.

The company opened the Quartermasters School to train military mechanics to work on motorcycles. The school converted to training civilian mechanics after the war.

Harley-Davidson bicycles hit the market for the first time.

1918   Half of the company's production was sold to the military.

1920   Harley-Davidson was the largest motorcycle company in the world, with dealers in 67 countries.

Harleys became known as "hogs" after winning factory racers carried their pig mascot on each victory lap.

1921   As more people bought cars, Harley sales plunged to the lowest point in 10 years. To cut costs, the factory closed down for a month, cut wages, and put the racing team on hold. Many factory race bikes were sold to European riders and some Harley riders headed overseas as well.

Alfred Rich Child rode the full length of Africa on a model J with sidecar to sell motorcycles and set up new dealerships.

Advertising began to target women as a new market. Advertising also began to play on the more indefinable qualities of freedom, individuality, and adventure.

1922   Harley-Davidson founders sat down with the management at rival Indian for the first of many price management meetings to keep prices steady in the face of a common enemy—the automobile.

Harley rolled out the 1,000 cc v-twin 74 to rival Indian's Big Chief.

1923   Arthur Davidson and a group of investors established the Kilbourn Finance Corporation to allow customers to buy Harleys on credit.

1924 Arthur Child set up the Harley-Davidson Motorcycle Sales Company of Japan with the Koto company in Tokyo, and began importing motorcycles and spare parts.

1925 Teardrop shape gas tanks replaced the old rectangular standards.

1926 Harley produced the 350 cc Peashooter in response to overseas market demands for a lighter racing bike. Both the racing version and a later street version enjoyed robust sales in Europe and eventually in the United States.

The company formed a separate department dedicated to police sales.

1927 Bessie Stringfield became the first African American woman to cross the United States on a motorcycle.

1928 Harley introduced the twin cam, 1200 cc JD 74 with a top speed of 100 miles per hour.

1000 cc and 1200 cc bikes got quieter mufflers, and all new models had front brakes for the first time.

1929 The 750 cc D 45 appeared on the scene, with two headlights and a fearsome horn. It would become known as the Flathead, one of Harley's most popular and reliable engines.

The stock market crashed in October, setting the stage for the Great Depression.

1931 Excelsior called it quit and closed down for good. Harley-Davidson's only competition was Indian.

The company offered chrome as a factory option.

1932 The 750 cc, three-wheel Servi-Car rolled out and was a hit with car dealers, garages, police forces, and delivery businesses.

The company offered paint color and detailing options on all models. It marked the official beginning of Harley-Davidson factory custom work.

1933 The U.S. economy had tanked out fully and Harley sold only 3,700 motorcycles that year.

To keep its people working, the company reduced hours, implemented work-sharing programs, dropped single-cylinder models, and produced motorcycles almost exclusively for overseas or commercial markets.

The art-deco eagle became standard on all gas tanks.

1934   Sales began to recover and went over 10,000 by the end of the year.

1935   Under a $75,000 licensing agreement, Japan produced its first motorcycles—Harleys with the name Rikuo.

1936   Harley introduced the 1000 cc Knucklehead. Also new were the 1000 cc and 1200 cc side valve workhorses that became a big hit with police departments.

1937   The Harley-Davidson shop became a union shop over fierce objections from the founders.

William Davidson died two days after signing the union agreement.

1939   War broke out again in Europe and Harley began supplying the Allies with motorcycles.

1941   The United States joined the war effort after Pearl Harbor, and Harley shifted production almost exclusively to military production. By the end of the war, Harley supplied the U.S. military and the Allies with 90,000 motorcycles.

The company service school began training army mechanics.

1942   Harley produced the XA 750 for desert use in North Africa. Only 1,000 were produced, and the contract was canceled when that part of the war ended.

Walter Davidson died. William's son, young Bill became president of the company.

1943   Bill Harley died. Arthur Davison was the last of the founders still standing.

1946   One-third of the bikes sold in the United States were imported from England. Bad omen.

1947   The company bought another building for a machine shop to produce parts.

The black leather jacket appeared in the Harley accessories catalogue for the first time.

1948 The Knucklehead got a make-over and became the Panhead, the precursor of the Evolution engines.

The company debuted a new lightweight 125 cc two-stroke single cylinder bike called the Hummer that got 90 miles to the gallon.

1949 The Panhead got hydraulic telescoping front forks and became known as the Hydra-Glide.

1950 Arthur Davidson and his wife were killed in a car wreck on December 30. The torch was passed to the next generation.

The British motorcycle invasion was in full swing, with their 250 cc and 500 cc bikes making a dent in Harley's market.

1951 The company failed to get Washington to impose a 40 percent tariff on imported motorcycles. Its own overseas sales were suffering from European high tariffs, yet European exporters faced very low U.S. tariffs.

1952 Harley introduced the K model, then the KH, and finally the KHK, all 750 cc machines, styled after the British bikes. They were no match in speed and performance and sold only moderately well.

1953 Harley celebrated its 50th anniversary.

The KR racing bike began to blow the British away at the racetracks.

Indian folded, leaving Harley as the only American motorcycle manufacturer.

1954 The movie *The Wild One* established the rebel biker image.

The Federal Trade Commission ordered Harley to cease its exclusivity demands on dealers. Harley dealers began stocking British-made motorcycles as well as Harleys.

1956 Elvis Presley appeared on the cover of the May issue of the Enthusiast riding his KH.

1957 The Sportster joined the Harley line-up and was an instant success. It was the first of the superbikes.

1958   The Hydra-Glide became the Duo-Glide, a first for both front and rear hydraulic suspensions and rear brakes.

1958–1959   Harley began design and production of the little run-about scooter called the Topper.

                    Negotiations began to buy into Italian motorcycle maker Aermacchi to import a 250 cc single-cylinder, 4-stroke bike to fill the middleweight niche in the Harley stable.

                    The Japanese began selling motorcycles in the United States.

1960   Harley-Davidson introduced the Topper, its first and only scooter, and its first use of fiberglass.

                    The Duo-Glide came in four performance levels, three iridescent colors, and a host of options including tinted windshields, saddlebags, and as much chrome as you wanted to slap on it.

                    The Sportster had two hot versions, one of them as close to a full-fledged race bike as you could legally get on the street.

1961   Harley debuted the Aermacchi-Harley-Davidson 250 cc Sprint. People weren't nearly as excited about it as they were about the first men in space. Some even went so far as to say if they wanted to buy a Harley, they wanted an American-made one—a real Harley.

1962   The 165 Hummer grew to 175 cc with three different versions—the Pacer for the street, the off-road Ranger, and the dual-purpose Scat.

                    Realizing the potential for using fiberglass in motorcycle production, the company bought a controlling share of the Tomahawk Boat Manufacturing Company.

                    Feeling it needed to broaden its markets, Harley began producing golf cars, both gas and electric. The first ones were three-wheelers. Four-wheelers came shortly after. By the end of the 1960s Harley had about a third of the golf car market cornered.

1963   Tomahawk became a fully operational division of Harley-Davidson.

                    Willie G. Davidson joined the company design department.

1964   The trusty Servi-Car became the first Harley with an electric starter.

1965   The Electra-Glide replaced the Duo-Glide and got an electric starter. So did the Sportster.

1966   Harley introduced the first Shovelhead engines on the Electra-Glide. They got their name because the cylinder covers looked like the working end of a shovel. They replaced the Panhead.

1969   The Sprint engine increased to 350 cc.

Harley-Davidson merged with American Machine and Foundry Company (AMF), essentially ending family ownership of the company.

1970   The street version of the Sportster XR 750 debuted with a red, white, and blue, one-piece fiberglass boat-tail seat/fender combo. The design was a resounding failure.

1971   The Sportster reappeared without the boat-tail and did well.

Willie G.'s FX Super-Glide hit the streets with the same boat-tail assembly as the Sportster and with the same ho-hum reception. It was the first of the custom cruisers inspired by the choppers and custom bike-builders.

Harley joined up with Evel Knievel, providing him with XR 750s for his widely televised jumps.

The AMF logo appeared on Harley tanks for the first time.

Harley began producing snowmobiles.

1972   The Super-Glide reappeared minus the boat-tail and was a resounding success.

The 1000 cc Sportster rolls off the line and is a hit.

The FLH Electra-Glide became the first factory-built motorcycle with both front and rear hydraulic brakes.

1973   Motorcycle and golf car assembly operations moved to the new plant in York, Pennsylvania. Several hundred workers in Milwaukee lost their jobs, and the union went on strike.

AMF dropped model names in favor of numbers and letters. Boy, did it get hard after that to keep up with which bike was which!

William Davidson (young Bill) left the company.

Sprints got electric starters.

Super-Glides got the tear drop gas tank to make them even sleeker.

1974   The Super-Glides got electric starters.

1975   The company quit making the Sprint.

1976   In honor of the country's bicentennial celebration, Harley put on its own display at Daytona Bike Week called "A Salute to American Motorcycling." It set up its show separately from the main exhibition tent and have continued that tradition ever since.

1977   The company again appealed to Washington for tariff relief in the face of the flood of Japanese heavyweights. Once again, Washington turned it down.

Willie G. presented his dragster-style FXS Low Rider at Daytona. It featured a low-slung seat, dragster handlebars, and distinctive paint job.

Late in the year, Willie G. came out with the Sportster-based Café Racer, but there weren't many takers, and the company dropped it the next year.

1978   Company president Vaughn Beals and a convoy of executives began a cross-country ride to celebrate Harley's 75th anniversary. It was also a goodwill ride, as they visited every dealership along the way and met with hundreds of customers and riders.

1979   Harley's best sales year ever. In spite of that, AMF had had enough and put the company up for sale.

Harley introduced the FXEF Fat Bob, named for its big dual gas tanks and bobbed rear fender. It was a smashing success.

1980   Harley debuted the smooth-riding 1300 cc FLT Tour Glide with a five-speed transmission and rubber-mounted drivetrain to cut down vibration. It also marked the return of the belt drive, this time Kevlar instead of the leather belts of the early days. Belt drives would become standard on all Harleys within a year or so.

In honor of the Sturgis Motorcycle Rally, Harley introduced the 1300 cc Sturgis model.

This was also the year of the Wide Glide. All three carried the distinctive mark of Willie G.'s custom styling.

1981 13 Harley executives offered a letter of intent to buy the company. The $81.5 million deal was closed in June. There was a celebratory ride from the York plant to Milwaukee with the rallying cry "The Eagle Soars Alone."

1982 With a new operating and management system in place, the quality of motorcycles and production efficiency improved by leaps and bounds. New confidence and innovative ideas led to the release of the Super Glide II, with its rubber-encased five-speed powertrain, and new upgrades to the Sportster.

1983 In response to the Japanese dumping a million or so heavy-weight bikes in the American market-place, Harley petitioned Washington for five-year tariff relief and got it.

The company began a series of PR moves to rebuild its image and draw riders and customers back to Harley. The first move was the formation of the Harley Owners Group (H.O.G.), with membership open to anyone who bought a Harley. Within a few years, membership grew to nearly 100,000.

SuperRide was another promotion that invited people to test ride a Harley at their nearest dealer. Tens of thousands of people came out for rides after the $3 million TV ad campaign.

1984 Harley released its boldest engine yet—the 1340 cc Evolution. It was fast, ran cooler, and didn't leak oil.

It also introduced the Softail model, named for its smooth-riding rear shock absorbers.

Harley won the contract to supply motorcycles for the California Highway Patrol. It was a signal that the quality of bikes had improved drastically.

1985 After losing $50 million over the first few years after the buyout, and saddled with enormous debt, the company headed to the brink of bankruptcy when their lender changed the terms of the buyout financing in 1984. At the last minute, Heller Financial Corporation stepped in to save the day.

1986   Sales climbed, and Harley offered 2 million shares of common stock for sale on the American Stock Exchange. It was the first time that Harley had been publicly traded since the AMF merger. The IPO brought in $25 million more than expected.

The whole Sportster line came out with the aluminum-alloy Evolution engine.

The Heritage Softail, with its Evolution engine and 1950s retro styling, debuted with great success.

1987   Harley was approved by the New York Stock Exchange and began trading under the ticker symbol HDI.

Harley petitioned the International Tariff Commission to end the tariffs on heavyweight motorcycles a year early.

The company began the buy-back program for the 883 cc Sportster, offering customers a full-value trade-in within two years if they decided to move up to a bigger model.

The company introduced the FLHS Electra Glide Sport, FLSTC Heritage Softail Classic, the FXLR Low Rider Custom, and to celebrate the 30th Anniversary of the Sportster, an 1100 cc version of their most popular motorcycle.

1988   Harley celebrated its 85th anniversary with the introduction of the biggest Sportster yet at 1200 cc.

Over 60,000 riders celebrated the anniversary at a big bash in Milwaukee.

The Springer Softail brought the return of the Springer front forks that had given way to hydraulics with the Hydra-Glide. This time, however, the Springer front end was the product of computer-assisted design and analysis.

The Harley-Davidson Traveling Museum began traveling around the country with displays of classic bikes and Harley memorabilia.

1989   Harley left the 1980s in style with a new line of touring bikes. This Ultra Classic line featured a new Tour Glide and

Electra-Glide with cruise control, glove box, four-speaker stereo systems with controls for both rider and passenger, and built-in CB radio.

1990   Willie G. rolled out his boldest custom bike yet—the FLSTF Fat Boy.

The international offices moved from Connecticut to Milwaukee, and the staff tripled. The company also opened a European parts and accessories warehouse in Germany.

1991   Exports had grown from 16 percent in 1987 to 30 percent by 1991. Leading export markets included Canada, West Germany, Japan, and Australia.

A new state-of-the-art paint shop opened in Milwaukee, reflecting the growing demand for custom motorcycles.

The Sportster got a five-speed transmission and the Dyna line debuted with the FXDB Dyna Glide Sturgis.

1993   Harley bought a small interest in Buell Motor-cycles to manufacture sport models using Sportster engines.

The new Dyna Wide Glide and the FLSTN Heritage Softail Nostalgia appeared in showrooms. The Nostalgia became known as the "Moo Glide" or "Cow Glide" because of all the cowhide accessories.

1994   The classic FLHR Road King debuts to rave reviews.

1995   To celebrate the 30th anniversary of the Electra-Glide, Harley put out the Ultra Classic, the first production bike with fuel injection.

The company began the Harley-Davidson Learning Center.

1996   Two new Sportsters were introduced—the Custom and the Sport.

The Parts and Accessories Distribution Center opened in Milwaukee, further implementing the company's plans for more efficiency and productivity.

A new plant opened in Kansas City, Missouri to help meet the rising demand for motorcycles. The whole process of locating, building, and staffing the plant was carried out under the company's new Partnering program.

1997   Jeff Bleustein took over as president from Rich Teerlink. Teerlink became chairman of the board.

1998   A new assembly plant opened in Manaus, Brazil, the first Harley plant outside the United States.

The company bought out Buell Motorcycles.

The Road Glide replaced the Tour Glide with a sleeker look and optional fuel-injected engine.

1999   The Touring and Dyna lines got new twin cam 88 engines.

Harley began three new programs—the Custom Vehicle Operations (CVO) department, the Harley-Davidson Authorized Rentals program and Rider's Edge.

The Buell Blast hit the showrooms and was an instant hit with the younger sporty crowd.

2000   The FXSTD Softail Deuce became an instant classic. All 2000 Softail models got the twin cam 88 engine and fuel injected engines.

2002   This was the year of the spectacular VRSCA V-Rod, based on the VR 1000 racer. It was the first bike that combined fuel injection, overhead cams, and a water-cooled engine. It put out 115 horsepower.

The new Buell Firebolt joined the Blast.

2003   The Buell Lightning rounded out the Buell line of sports bikes.

The company celebrated its 100th anniversary in style as more than 200,000 bikers came to the four-day party in Milwaukee. Harley enthusiasts all over the world threw their own parties.

2004   The Sportster line got rubber engines mounts for less vibration, new frames, and bigger rear tires.

The FLHRSI Road King Custom joined the big bike line-up.

2005   The FLSTNI Softail Deluxe and the Springer Softail Classic brought back memories of the 1930s and 1940s with chopper custom features.

Jeff Bleustein passed the torch to Jim Ziemer and moved over to chairman of the board.

Harley and the Muscular Dystrophy Association celebrated their 25-year partnership.

2006 The Dyna line got six-speed transmissions, and the Street Bob joined the family. The Street Glide joined the Touring line.

Harley opened its first dealership in mainland China.

2007 Union workers at the York, Pennsylvania plant called a strike that lasted for over three weeks. It led to layoffs in Milwaukee and the company scaling back its forecasts for motorcycle deliveries and revenues.

Engine Development Timeline

FLATHEAD

1909–1936   The Flathead got its name from the flat, vented tops on each cylinder head. This was the engine that powered the Harley racing team to one victory after another in the 1920s. A typical Flathead engine had a displacement of 45 cubic inches (742 cc) and produced about 22 horsepower.

KNUCKLEHEAD

1936–1947   The Knucklehead got its name from the knobby bumps on the valve covers. It carried the company and the U.S. military through the wars. The Knucklehead came in 60 cubic inch (990 cc) and 74 cubic inch (1200 cc) variations that produced 40 and 45 horsepower, respectively.

PANHEAD

1948–1965   The Panhead featured hydraulic valve lifters and got its name from the valve covers that looked like upside down cake pans. The Panhead also came in 60 cubic inch (990 cc) and 74 cubic inch (1200 cc) variations that produced 50 and 55 horsepower, respectively. Unlike the Knucklehead, the Panhead had aluminum heads instead of cast iron.

SHOVELHEAD

1966–1983   The Shovelhead had a distinctive enclosed cylinder head with a sleek, slightly curved top. It sort of looked like the working end of a shovel. Shovelheads displaced 74 cubic inches (1200 cc) and produced 60 horsepower.

EVOLUTION

1983–1999   This redesign of the v-twin used styled, square blocks to house the valve train and got the nickname Blockhead. The Evolution engine was the first of many quality improvements after the buyout from AMF in 1981. For the first time, Harleys didn't leak oil. Displacement was 81.8 cubic inches (1340 cc), and produced 70 horsepower.

TWIN CAM 88

1999–Present   The Twin Cam 88 is Harley's most revolutionary engine yet. The Twin Cam 88 gets its name from its two cams versus the single cam in all its ancestors. With 88 cubic inches (1450 cc) of displacement, it produces 80 horsepower. The engine remains air-cooled, and uses overhead valves. It's also called the Fathead because of its bigger heads. That was a no-brainer, wasn't it?

REVOLUTION

2001–Present   The Revolution engine is currently used on only one Harley production model—the VSRC. It is a water-cooled v-twin but differs from the other v-twins in the angle of the cylinders. The standard v-twin is 45 degrees, while the Revolution is 60 degrees. It has four overhead cams and is fuel injected. It is a smaller, high revving engine—only 69 cubic inches (1130 cc), producing 115 horsepower.

Selected Bibliography

BOOKS

Bolfert, Thomas. *The Big Book of Harley-Davidson: Centennial Edition.* Official Publication by Harley-Davidson Motor Company. Milwaukee, WI: Motorbooks International, 2002.

Davidson, Jean. *Jean Davidson's Harley-Davidson Family Album.* Stillwater, MN: Voyageur Press, Inc., 2003

Davidson, Willie G. *100 Years of Harley Davidson.* New York: Bullfinch Press, 2002.

Girdler, Allan, and Jeff Hackett (with Bob Woods). *Harley-Davidson.* St. Paul, MN: Motorbooks, 2006.

Green, William. *Harley-Davidson: The Living Legend.* New York: Crescent Books, 1993.

Harley-Davidson, Inc. *Historical Overview 1903–1993.* Milwaukee, WI: Harley-Davidson, Inc., 1994

Norris, Martin. *Rolling Thunder.* Philadelphia, PA: Courage Books, 1992.

Rafferty, Tod. *Harley-Davidson: The Ultimate Machine, 100th Anniversary Edition 1903–2003.* Philadelphia, PA: Courage Books, 2002.

Reid, Peter C. *Well Made in America: Lessons from Harley-Davidson on Being the Best.* New York: McGraw-Hill, 1990.

Supple, Jack. *100 Years of Harley-Davidson Advertising.* New York: Bullfinch Publishing, 2002.

Teerlink, Rich, and Ozley Lee. *More Than a Motorcycle: The Leadership Journey at Harley-Davidson.* Boston: Harvard Business School Press, 2000

Wagner, Herbert. *Harley-Davidson, 1930–1941: Revolutionary Motorcycles and Those Who Rode Them.* Atglen, PA: Schiffer Publishing, 1996.

Williams, Mark (photographs by Garry Stuart). *The Classic Harley.* New York: Smithmark, 1993.

MAGAZINES

American Rider, http://www.americanrider.com.
Motorcycle Cruiser, PRIMEDIA, Los Angeles, CA.
Motorcycle Encyclopedia, http://www.bikez.com/.

WEB SITES

The Harley-Davidson Web Site, http://www.harley-davidson.com. This is a rich resource about the company, including history, racing, financials and investor information, setting up a dealership, all their programs for riders and owners, and, of course, tons and tons of stuff about the bikes.

How Stuff Works, http://howstuffworks.com. This is a fantastic Web site with information about how all kinds of stuff works. They have a huge section devoted to Harley, with data on bikes, engines, performance, and styling organized by years with all makes and models. It's a great site for digging a little deeper into the workings of a Harley. Lots of photos, too.

Index

About the Author

MISSY SCOTT, a former broadcast journalist, is a freelance writer and instructional designer. She writes courseware and supporting materials for teachers in college, universities, and healthcare training schools. She is coauthor of *In Defiance of Death: Exposing the Real Costs of End of Life Care* (Praeger 2007).